MW01514231

In the Lap of God

In the Lap of God

Comfort From the Psalms

Michael Gifford

HOPKINS
publishing inc.

All Scripture quotations, unless otherwise noted, are taken from the Holy Bible, King James Version, Cambridge, 1769.

HOPKINS
publishing inc.

P.O. Box 3687
Cleburne, TX 76033
HopkinsPublishing.com

Copyright © 2013 Michael Gifford
ISBN-13: 978-1-62080-975-4
Library of Congress Control Number: 2013940125
Version 1.0

All rights reserved. No part of this book may be reproduced or transmitted in any form or by any means without written permission from the publisher, except for the inclusion of short quotations or as otherwise provided by applicable copyright laws. Above all, remember that you will stand in judgment before God for every word and every action (Matthew 12:36). Act accordingly, making sure to keep a clear conscience.

Discover Other Titles
By Hopkins Publishing
HopkinsPublishing.com

Dedicated to my Shannon
I will see her again.
I Thessalonians 4:13-18

Contents

Introduction ....*ix*

Part One
Psalms with Themes of Comfort..1

Chapter One
From the Depths 3
Chapter Two
Psalm 1 The Comfort of Stability 7
Chapter Three
Psalm 3 Comfort In the Strength and Protection of God............13
Chapter Four
Psalm 22 Comfort In the Messianic Promise 17
Chapter Five
Psalm 23 The Comfort of Realizing that the Shepherd Knows Me
and I Know the Shepherd...23
Chapter Six
Psalm 29 The Comfort of Knowing That God Is In Control 29
Chapter Seven
Psalm 34 The Comfort of God-fearing Fearlessness 33
Chapter Eight
Psalm 73 The Comfort of God's Patience 37
Chapter Nine
Psalm 77 The Comfort of Remembering 43
Chapter Ten
Psalm 84 Comfort "At the End of the Day" 49

Chapter Eleven
Psalm 91
Comfort In Knowing That Nothing Can Really Harm Us...........53
Chapter Twelve
Psalm 93 The Comfort of Knowing That God is Bigger Than Our
Troubles 57
Chapter Thirteen
Psalm 95 The Comfort of Fellowship In Worship........................61
Chapter Fourteen
Psalm 102 Comfort In Prayer..65
Chapter Fifteen
Psalm 103 Comfort In Forgiveness...71
Chapter Sixteen
Psalm 116 Comfort In Persistence..75
Chapter Seventeen
Psalm 118 The Comfort of Knowing That I Will Win.................79
Chapter Eighteen
Psalm 120 Comfort Even In the Presence of Evil Influences........85
Chapter Nineteen
Psalm 121 Comfort In God's Preservation..................................89
Chapter Twenty
Psalm 130 Comfort In Waiting For the Lord..............................93
Chapter Twenty-One
Psalm 139 Comfort "24/7/365" 99
Chapter Twenty-Two
Psalm 142 Comfort In My Refuge 103

Part Two
Individual Verses of Comfort.. 107
Part Three
Personally Sitting in the Lap of God.. 123
Appendix
God's Plan of Salvation 145

Introduction

May 27, 2009 is a day that will stand out in my mind for the rest of my life. Just one week earlier my beautiful wife, Shannon had undergone what we had understood was to be nothing more than routine surgery. I can still see her getting into the van after her follow-up appointment at the doctor's office on May 27. She asked me to pull over because we needed to talk. In the next few moments I would hear the words that everyone dreads as she calmly said, "The doctor told me that I have cancer." At 49 years of age and her at 51, I was not expecting to hear such news. We were "supposed to" enjoy a long life together, walking hand in hand into our winter years, playing with grandchildren and growing old together. How could it be possible that my wife had developed a disease that had the potential to take her away from me far too soon?

As you would expect, tears flowed when we went home and told our children of their mother's diagnosis. We certainly weren't going to give cancer the victory over our spirits or over her life but we knew that we had a battle ahead of us. Besides that, the mere thought of one whom we loved so much having something wrong with her was unnerving.

Life was relatively calm for about six weeks as we awaited the next surgery. Following it, another month went by without much incident. Then the bottom started to drop out as the cancer spread and began affecting other parts of her body. The next eight months were filled with ambulance rides, hospital stays, emergency room visits, doctor appointments, tests, pills, shots and a host of procedures and treatments. Finally, as April 2010 dawned, Shannon was sent home from the hospital. There was nothing else that could be done other than to make her comfortable in the few weeks the doctors suggested she had left. On April 18, 2010 at 8:59 p.m. Eastern time, Shannon Gifford went home to be with the Lord. I was with her as she died; holding her hand and gazing intently at the face I would never again see on this side of eternity.

Other family members were there as well. Each of us shared our expressions of love with her and she shared hers with us. Shannon and I exchanged one last loving look into each other's eyes. She then closed her eyes to this world for the final time, only to reopen them in the next world and see the smiling face of the Lord in Paradise. It was a storybook ending to a life well lived as a wife, a mother, a Bible class teacher and a faithful Christian who understood what it meant to be a servant to the Lord and to others.

Throughout the challenges we faced over the eleven month period of her illness, we found ourselves in study of God's Word. This was nothing new as we both had been reared by faithful Christian parents. After we were married, Bible reading and prayer were daily privileges in our home. During the time of her illness we would frequently find ourselves in the Psalms. While Psalm 23 and its glorious picture of passing through the valley of the shadow of death with the Shepherd's protection were often discussed, it was not the only Psalm that brought us comfort. We found many that set our hearts at ease as together we faced Shannon's disease. A desire to share the marvelous comfort we found in the Psalms is the motivation behind this book.

Several years ago a Gospel preacher friend of mine by the name of Delbert Carver lost his wife. It so happened that I was teaching a Wednesday night adult Bible class on the Psalms at that time and Delbert attended. Many times throughout that class and in fact many times throughout the ensuing years prior to his own death, he would tell me, "I was in great sorrow when my wife died. When you taught the class on the Psalms, you made me feel like I was sitting in the lap of God." That statement is the origin of the title of this book.

The apostle Paul wrote in II Corinthians 1:3-4, "*Blessed be God, even the Father of our Lord Jesus Christ, the Father of mercies, and the God of all comfort; who comforteth us in all our tribulation, that we may be able to comfort them which are in any trouble, by the comfort wherewith we ourselves are comforted of God.*" Paul received his comfort from God, but he did not keep it to himself. He freely and gladly used the serenity he found in God as a tool for helping others experience the same peace. That is my purpose in writing this book.

The book is divided into three sections. Part one takes a look at twenty-one different Psalms that in their overall theme can bring comfort to the troubled heart. Part two offers a categorical listing of around 200 individual verses of comfort from the Psalms. Part three contains information that, at first, I wasn't sure should be included. It includes a great deal of personal material regarding our struggle with cancer. At the urging of friends I added this section in the hopes that others dealing with this dreadful disease might be able to identify with the challenges Shannon and I faced and overcame.

When I began my research, my desire was to write the definitive uninspired work on comfort in the Psalms. As each chapter unfolded I found that this was not feasible. There are so many situations in which we need comfort and each of these situations is multi-faceted. I can write from the perspective of my pain, but beyond that I am rather helpless. I can't begin to fathom the anguish that some have felt nor, for that matter, can some grasp what I feel. That being the case, I have written this from the vantage point of one Christian and the comfort he gained from the Psalms. Perhaps the sadness we all experience in our lives is generic enough that the words herein will touch at least a portion of the hearts of all who read. Besides, my words are not the emphasis. God's Word is the focus and it can aid all who need Divine comfort.

May your troubles be eased by the inspired words of the Psalms as much as they comforted Shannon and me during our life together and as much as they comfort me now that she and I are apart. "*Beloved, I wish above all things that thou mayest prosper and be in health, even as thy soul prospereth.*" (III John 2).

Michael Gifford
November 2010

Part One
Psalms with Themes of Comfort

Chapter One
From the Depths

When coming face to face with life's challenges, the afflicted individual often measures the words of comfort from friends and family by this one primary thought: "Have you felt what I'm feeling now?" While another's warm touch, sympathizing tear and gentle word can indeed help the troubled soul, there is nothing like talking to someone who has "been there." God demonstrated His understanding of this principle in sending the Son to take on a fleshly body. *"For in that he himself hath suffered being tempted, he is able to succour them that are tempted."* (Hebrews 2:18). In the Psalms, God inspired His writers to occasionally tell us something of the depths of their sorrows and struggles. These were not men who were spouting empty platitudes from ivory towers. Each one of them had waged a personal war against despair, poured forth the tears of anguish and begged from shattered hearts for comfort from the Father.

How many of us have ever cried like this: *"I am weary with my groaning; all the night make I my bed to swim; I water my couch with my tears. Mine eye is consumed because of grief; it waxeth old because of all mine enemies."* (Psalm 6:6-7). This was not intermittent shedding of tears brought about by moments of sadness. This was, as we might say today, "bawling your eyes out." David's crying was so intense that it was literally draining him of physical strength. His vision was diminished due to the cloudiness of the tears. The severity of his heartache was so great that crying alone could not express it; groans flowed from his lips in unison with the tears. If you have hurt like David then you know how he felt. Perhaps your tears have been so strong that your stomach ached or your head hurt. Perhaps your crying had so weakened you that you could not eat. Perhaps you even cried yourself to sleep. You have a friend in the inspired Psalmist for even if the cause of his suffering might not have been the same as yours, he was well acquainted with sorrow's tears.

Closely connected to the Psalmists' tears were their feelings of being overwhelmed by their circumstances. Psalm 69 begins, "*Save me, O God; for the waters are come in unto my soul. I sink in deep mire, where there is no standing: I am come into deep waters, where the floods overflow me.*" (verses 1-2). This is a poignant word picture of one who feels like he has lost control. Not only is he being pulled down by the undertow of the rivers of sorrow, but the dike of protection has burst and the flood waters of despair have come crashing down on top of him. He has no footing but is sinking deeper and deeper into the mire. As those who have experienced suffering identify with this feeling we might think of how in our tragedy everything seemed to come upon us at once. When earlier in life, perhaps just a few days or hours earlier, everything was running smoothly and pleasantly, suddenly we found ourselves being bombarded on every side with emotions, thoughts and new directions in life that heretofore would have never even crossed our minds. We could barely think straight. Conversations with others were like dreams filled with empty words that passed over our heads and never touched our ears. So much was happening all at once that we could ourselves have felt those stressful waters of Psalm 69 rushing over our heads.

In many of the Psalms we find the writers turning immediately to God, praising and honoring Him. In some of them, however, while they eventually turned to God, initially they expressed their concerns about God's care for them. The inspired writer of Psalm 13 opened this particular poem with the questions, "*How long will thou forget me, O Lord? for ever? how long wilt thou hide thy face from me?*" Had God deserted this writer? He certainly had not, but in the Psalmist's anguish he felt that the one on whom he had learned to depend had in fact turned His back to the trouble and forgotten His servant. Why doesn't God answer? Why did He let this happen to me? What possible good can come from all of this? Such expressions are as evident in the hearts of sufferers today as they were when this Psalmist penned his questions. Is there anyone who, in their grief, has not at least once asked, "Why?" This simple, one word question is not necessarily a challenge to God nor is it necessarily an indication of a lack of faith. It could instead be a reflection of our imperfection, our inability to see and fully know the mind of God. It's possible that on earth we may never fully know why. That is not a tragedy. Ceasing to draw closer to God is the tragedy.

Much more could be said about the depths of despair from which the Psalmists often wrote but in these few short paragraphs we can see in these men's lives an affirmative answer to the question with which this chapter opened: "Have you felt what I'm feeling now?" Indeed they did experience these feelings and in writing by perfect inspiration of the Holy Spirit, they have shown their words to be worthy of our consideration as we seek the comfort from the Lord that lifted them from their sorrows.

The circumstances behind each Psalm may be different than ours, but the pain is just as real. It may not be death or illness that triggers our sorrow. There are countless difficulties in life that could prompt tears and heartache. The fact is though that every sorrow bears the same characteristic. It hurts. No matter what has caused our hearts to become heavy, even if it's something that would seem trivial to others, it still hurts and we still want relief. In reading these Psalms, we can see others who themselves have felt this pain and, in studying their inspired words, it's as though we were walking hand in hand with them, facing life's troubles and looking up for the comfort that they found, and that we ourselves can find, in the Lord.

Chapter Two
Psalm 1
The Comfort of Stability

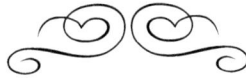

1Blessed is the man that walketh not in the counsel of the ungodly, nor standeth in the way of sinners, nor sitteth in the seat of the scornful.

2But his delight is in the law of the Lord; and in his law doth he meditate day and night.

3And he shall be like a tree planted by the rivers of water, that bringeth forth his fruit in his season; his leaf also shall not wither; and whatsoever he doeth shall prosper.

4The ungodly are not so: but are like the chaff which the wind driveth away.

5Therefore the ungodly shall not stand in the judgment, nor sinners in the congregation of the righteous.

6For the Lord knoweth the way of the righteous: but the way of the ungodly shall perish.

In the summer of 1988 I was participating in a Bible lectureship in the Pacific islands. During one of the lectures the ground began to rumble and the structures started to shake. For the first time in my life I was experiencing an earthquake. The locals, having been through these disturbances countless times, probably enjoyed the entertainment of watching at least this one American frantically scanning the area for something to grab for support. They knew full well, as I myself soon realized, that nothing above the ground would provide stability as long as the ground itself was quaking uncontrollably. The very foundation upon which we stood having become unstable, we could not expect anything that rested upon this faulty foundation to be trustworthy.

When tragedy strikes and our lives tumble in, we can easily identify with the feeling of helplessness that comes with being in an earthquake. Things are no longer as they once were. People upon whom we depended are no longer within our reach. The temporal, shaky nature of this earthly life is never more evident than when trials beset us. We can stretch with all of our might in an effort to grab hold of something here on earth that is rock solid and immovable, but we will only grasp air. Where is that stability that we so desperately crave when our world is crumbling? Where is that constant to which we can cling when the tides of sorrow are threatening to sweep us away? Is it even possible for us to regain our balance or are we doomed to live a life of continual sadness and despair?

How appropriate that this first Psalm opens with the word, "blessed" or "happy." By the use of some powerful illustrations and statements, it declares that this happiness is found in the stability that was mentioned earlier, that precious commodity that all of mankind desires, especially when we're in the grip of tragedy.

The third verse paints the picture of stability for us as it describes a healthy and prosperous tree. Notice that this is not a tree that has grown up in the wild, nor is it one that has come up from a mere scattering of seed from a farmer's hand. This tree has been planted. Furthermore, it has been planted thoughtfully and purposefully in a location that is well-watered, thus giving it the best opportunity to be productive. With such tender care given it in its early days, the tree sinks its roots deeply into the rich soil and grounds itself firmly. As it gains strength in its foundation, it bears fruit in abundance and does not wither or fade even during the stress of the hottest of days, the bitterest of wintry temperatures or the harshest of winds. It is steadfast and unshakable.

The fourth verse again demonstrates stability, though from a negative perspective. Here the picture is of a farmer winnowing his grain. He tosses the grain into the air and while the heavier kernels fall to the ground, the lighter husks or chaff are carried away with the wind. While the emphasis in the verse is on the chaff that is blown away, the analogy bears the implication that there were also desirable grains that were landing where they were supposed to. Instability is pictured in the chaff and soundness and positive expectations are pictured in the kernels of the grain.

Yet another reference to stability is found in the sixth verse in which the Psalmist speaks of the Lord knowing the way of the righteous. One fact is certain when tragedy comes into our lives: We are traveling a new and unknown path. To be sure, we might have faced similar situations in the past, but no two challenges are exactly alike. For example, while the loss of a parent to death is bitterly painful, no one can begin to compare it to the loss of a spouse. While the death of a spouse brings unspeakable sorrow, no one can compare this to the loss of a child. It's not possible for anyone to rank sorrow as though one type were worse than another. The point is that each difficulty carries its own weight of heartache and grief. Each is a new experience. Each is an unknown way for us as humans, but *the Lord knoweth the way of the righteous.* God knows the way. He is the constant in the uncertainty that tragedy brings with it.

The aforementioned verses show that stability does indeed exist. Further, this stability can be attained by us, even when we're wrestling with life's most formidable challenges. But is stability going to show itself voluntarily without any effort on our part? Can we expect to be standing in the darkest of despair's shadows one day and automatically be catapulted by some unknown force into the brightest of life's joys the next?

Look again at verse three and notice that this entire verse shows a result. It depicts the end of a means. The means is found in verses one and two. The person described in those two verses is one who does not walk in the counsel of the ungodly, does not stand in the way of sinners and does not sit in the seat of the scornful (arrogant, haughty). This individual does, however, delight in the law of the Lord and meditates therein day and night. This is the reason why he is like a tree planted by the rivers of water. He seeks God and loves His Word. Even though there are things in life that threaten his fruitfulness and spiritual prosperity, he enjoys stability because he is firmly grounded in the one who Himself is the essence of stability, namely, Jehovah God. Just as the farmer purposefully planted the tree in a rich and beneficial location, the individual who enjoys God's stability has purposefully planted himself or herself in the rich and spiritually beneficial firm foundation of God's inspired Word.

Now look again at verse four. Who is it who gets blown away like the chaff? Who is it who will never know the stability that God offers through His Word? It is the ungodly man or woman who cannot stand and who will not stand. In fact, verse five clearly shows that those who turn away from God have no foundation at all. When their world quakes uncontrollably, they have nothing solid onto which they can grab because their ungodly foundation is the cause of their instability.

Our stability depends upon us turning to God for He is stability defined. He is eternal (Psalm 90:2), which means He was in existence before the world began. He was there in the beginning of the world, He Himself being the Creator (Genesis 1). He is ever present each second, He Himself being the sustainer of His creation (Jeremiah 23:23-24). He will be there at the end of the world, He Himself being the one who will destroy the elements (II Peter 3:10-12) and judge mankind (Matthew 25:31-46). He was there when the Bible began to be written (II Timothy 3:16-17). He gave each word of the Bible to His inspired writers (I Corinthians 2:7-15). He will be there in the end to employ His Word in judgment (Revelation 20:12). He was there at the beginning of each of our lives (Psalm 139:13). He is with us on a moment by moment basis (Hebrews 13:5). He will be with us at the end of our days (Psalm 23). Daily, He is there when we rise in the morning (Psalm 5:3), He is there with us throughout the day (Matthew 6:25-34), He is there with us when the day is done (Psalm 4:8) and then He is there with us all through the night (Psalm 121:4).

God's stability is demonstrated in His faithfulness to mankind, faithfulness that can be seen on page after page of His written Word. It's there in Genesis where we learn of mankind's fall into sin and then the immediate introduction of God's plan for redeeming man (Genesis 3:15). It's found throughout the books of the Law, from the rest of Genesis through Deuteronomy, as the Lord frees Israel from Egyptian bondage, thus ultimately portraying spiritual freedom from sin in Jesus Christ and then as He leads Israel to the earthly promised land of Canaan, a portrayal of the Christian's walk through the wilderness of this world to the eternal promised land of heaven. It's in the Old Testament books of history, from Joshua through Esther where God is constantly involved in the affairs of Israel and Judah. It's in the books of poetry from Job to Song of Solomon in which inspired writers tell us of God's deliverance and dependability. It's in the words of the Old Testament prophets, from Isaiah through Malachi where one inspired man after another continues the theme of eternal redemption begun in Genesis by foretelling the coming of the Messiah to pay the price for the sins of mankind. It's in the Gospel accounts of the New Testament where we read of the actual physical arrival of Jesus, God in the flesh (John 1:14), His perfect life and His death, burial and resurrection. It's in the book of Acts where we find men like Stephen finding the Lord faithful to him even in death (Acts 7). It's in the New Testament epistles, from Romans through Jude, in which we find an abundance of precious promises all given by our God who cannot lie (Titus 1:2). It's in the book of Revelation and its powerful portrait of victory in heaven for the faithful, provided by the one whose "*sayings are faithful and true.*" (Revelation 22:6).

We can have the stability that brings comfort when it seems our world is falling to pieces. We can be the firmly planted tree and the weighted grain. We can walk confidently upon the shifting sands of life if we are walking with the one who knows the way.

Chapter Three
Psalm 3
Comfort In the Strength and Protection of God

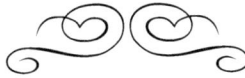

1Lord, how are they increased that trouble me! many are they that rise up against me.

2Many there be which say of my soul, There is no help for him in God. Selah.

3But thou, O Lord, art a shield for me; my glory, and the lifter up of mine head.

4I cried unto the Lord with my voice, and he heard me out of his holy hill. Selah.

5I laid me down and slept; I awaked; for the Lord sustained me.

6I will not be afraid of ten thousands of people, that have set themselves against me round about.

7Arise, O Lord; save me, O my God: for thou hast smitten all mine enemies upon the cheek bone; thou hast broken the teeth of the ungodly.

8Salvation belongeth unto the Lord: thy blessing is upon thy people. Selah.

The caption of this Psalm, though not Divinely inspired, suggests that it was written by King David when he fled from his son, Absalom. A full account of this can be found in II Samuel, chapters 15 through 18. In essence, Absalom deceived the Israelites and caused David to be run out of the land (II Samuel 15:13-14). David's own son turned the people against the mighty king. The sixth verse of this Psalm might be hyperbole, but then again perhaps it's not such a stretch to imagine Absalom having poisoned tens of thousands of hearts against David.

Verses six and seven form the basis for making the claim that this is a Psalm of comfort. Considering his circumstances, how could David possibly sleep well at night and walk without fear during the day? Aren't feelings of panic and desperation often associated with the onslaught of troubles? Aren't worry and doubt those insidious thieves that typically rob us of sleep and inner peace when we're faced with difficulties? These were not a part of David's mindset though for he knew that the God of all creation was taking care of him. Even though his enemies had "increased," were "many" in number and were even mocking him, saying, "*There is no help for him in God*," this sweet psalmist of Israel (II Samuel 23:1) enjoyed peace of mind. Though his detractors should gang up in the tens of thousands against him, David would not fear because His trust was in the all powerful God. No matter how many would rise up against him, he knew he would be the victor with his hand in the hand of the Lord.

In verse three, David portrays God as a shield. The American Standard Version translates this phrase, "*But thou, Jehovah, art a shield about me,*" the word "about" suggesting that God had covered him in protection. In the same verse the writer refers to God as "my glory." Even though this phrase is variously explained, it seems that since David was honoring God in the context, he was indicating that God was the source of his glory or honor. Being that source, He could be counted on to care for David no matter how severe the attacks that might be aimed at him. Again in verse three, David identified God as "*the lifter up of mine head.*" This could have referred to God keeping David's head up in hope rather than down in despair or it could have been a prophecy of David's return to power in Israel. In either case, the Lord was the one who had the strength to accomplish these tasks. It was his confidence in this Divine strength that prompted David to cry unto the Lord and it was his knowledge of God having heard his cry that led to his restful nights and fear-free days.

Have any of us ever had tens of thousands of people after us? Have we ever been so beset by enemies that we had to run for our lives? Perhaps not, but if we have experienced difficulties in our lives, we are familiar with the feeling that practically everything and everyone is against us.

Have you ever made these comments to yourself? "Nothing ever goes my way." "Nothing ever works out for me." "It's not fair." "This isn't supposed to be happening to me." Real or imagined, these feelings hurt and can lead to the worry and doubt mentioned earlier. Is there nothing we can do about our situation? Is there no one who can help us? Yes, there is a shield and "lifter up of the head" who demonstrates His strength to protect just as powerfully as he did in the days of king David.

The last nine verses of the eighth chapter of Romans go hand in hand with the message of God's protection in the third Psalm. Together these verses form a beautiful segment of inspired Scripture that remind us of the amazing ability of our God to provide the strength we need in times of trouble.

In the context, Paul is writing in regard to suffering being experienced by Christians in Rome. Romans 8:31 asks, *"What shall we then say to these things* (the suffering, mg)? *If God be for us, who can be against us?"* Immediately we see the power of God in these two simple questions. No matter how great the challenges of life may become, nothing can capture and enslave us if we are walking with God. None of life's tribulations can rule our hearts when our hearts are shielded by the Lord.

Reading on, we find Paul reminding Christians of the extent to which God had gone to show his loving care. He had given His only begotten Son. This is called an argument from the greater to the lesser. Since God was willing to send Jesus to die for the sins of mankind, why should we think that He would not take care of and protect us on a daily basis?

Then Paul comes to his magnificent conclusion. Read it, memorize it, internalize it and let these Divinely inspired words lead you through the dark valley of life's challenges.

> Who shall separate us from the love of Christ? shall tribulation, or distress, or persecution, or famine, or nakedness, or peril, or sword? As it is written, For thy sake we are killed all the day long; we are accounted as sheep for the slaughter. Nay, in all these things we are more than conquerors through him that loved us. For I am persuaded, that neither death, nor life, nor angels, nor principalities, nor powers, nor things present, nor things to come, Nor height, nor depth, nor any other creature, shall be able to separate us from the love of God, which is in Christ Jesus our Lord. (Romans 8:35-39).

Satan would have us believe that there is no help in God. He would raise tens of thousands of doubts and distresses in our minds. God is our strength and protection against the fiery darts of the devil (Ephesians 6:16). Like David, we too can say in our trials, "*the Lord sustained* (supported, mg) *me.*"

Chapter Four
Psalm 22
Comfort In the Messianic Promise

1My God, my God, why hast thou forsaken me? why art thou so far from helping me, and from the words of my roaring?

2O my God, I cry in the daytime, but thou hearest not; and in the night season, and am not silent.

3But thou art holy, O thou that inhabitest the praises of Israel.

4Our fathers trusted in thee: they trusted, and thou didst deliver them.

5They cried unto thee, and were delivered: they trusted in thee, and were not confounded.

6But I am a worm, and no man; a reproach of men, and despised of the people.

7All they that see me laugh me to scorn: they shoot out the lip, they shake the head, saying,

8He trusted on the Lord that he would deliver him: let him deliver him, seeing he delighted in him.

9But thou art he that took me out of the womb: thou didst make me hope when I was upon my mother's breasts.

10I was cast upon thee from the womb: thou art my God from my mother's belly.

11Be not far from me; for trouble is near; for there is none to help.

12Many bulls have compassed me: strong bulls of Bashan have beset me round.

13They gaped upon me with their mouths, as a ravening and a roaring lion.

14I am poured out like water, and all my bones are out of joint: my heart is like wax; it is melted in the midst of my bowels.

15My strength is dried up like a potsherd; and my tongue cleaveth to my jaws; and thou hast brought me into the dust of death.

16For dogs have compassed me: the assembly of the wicked have inclosed me: they pierced my hands and my feet.

17I may tell all my bones: they look and stare upon me.

18They part my garments among them, and cast lots upon my vesture.

19But be not thou far from me, O Lord: O my strength, haste thee to help me.

20Deliver my soul from the sword; my darling from the power of the dog.

21Save me from the lion's mouth: for thou hast heard me from the horns of the unicorns.

22I will declare thy name unto my brethren: in the midst of the congregation will I praise thee.

23Ye that fear the Lord, praise him; all ye the seed of Jacob, glorify him; and fear him, all ye the seed of Israel.

24For he hath not despised nor abhorred the affliction of the afflicted; neither hath he hid his face from him; but when he cried unto him, he heard.

25My praise shall be of thee in the great congregation: I will pay my vows before them that fear him.

26The meek shall eat and be satisfied: they shall praise the Lord that seek him: your heart shall live for ever.

27All the ends of the world shall remember and turn unto the Lord: and all the kindreds of the nations shall worship before thee.

28For the kingdom is the Lord's: and he is the governor

among the nations.
29All they that be fat upon earth shall eat and worship: all
they that go down to the dust shall bow before him: and none
can keep alive his own soul.
30A seed shall serve him; it shall be accounted to the Lord
for a generation.
31They shall come, and shall declare his righteousness unto a
people that shall be born, that he hath done this.

The comfort we receive from the Lord while here on earth is tremendous. Psalm 94:19 says, "*In the multitude of my thoughts within me thy comforts delight my soul.*" The hearts and minds of faithful Christians are sustained daily by God's great mercy and care. Beyond this earthly realm however is eternal comfort. Thoughts of eternity with God elicit moments of peace as we contemplate the land beyond where "*there shall be no more death, neither sorrow, nor crying, neither shall there be any more pain: for the former things are passed away.*" (Revelation 21:4). The ultimate comfort is heaven. This Psalm prophesies of the one whose suffering and death opened the way to heaven so that we can enjoy this hope here on earth and peace and comfort in eternity.

The Psalm opens with a plaintive cry from one whose anguish is so deep that he considers that God has turned a blind eye to his pain and a deaf ear to his pleas for help. His calamitous state is further seen in verses 6-8 and 16-18. Were this just the writer himself bemoaning his sorrowful situation, we would be sufficiently touched to feel for him and to pity his poor condition. However, when we come to the New Testament and find that these verses are prophecies of none other than Jesus Christ Himself during His suffering up to and while on the cross, we realize the depth of the heartache felt by our Lord while He walked the earth in human flesh. That He Himself suffered is enough to make us weep, but that He suffered due to no sin of His own is not only enough to make us weep, but also to thank God for the temporal suffering Jesus endured so that we might avoid eternal suffering in hell.

The Messianic prophecies of Psalm 22 find their fulfillment in the events recorded in Matthew, Mark, Luke and John. Psalm 22:1 is uttered by Jesus while He hung on the cross (Matthew 27:46; Mark 15:34). Psalm 22:6-8 describe in perfect prophetic fashion the surrounding scene of human indecency as Jesus was giving His life's blood for our sins (Matthew 27:39-44; Mark 15:29-32; Luke 23:35-37). Psalm 22:16 foretells the piercing of the Christ (Matthew 27:35; Mark 15:25; Luke 23:33; John 19:18; 20:24-27) while Psalm 22:17-18 give more details regarding the actions of the onlookers at the cross (Matthew 27:35; Mark 15:24; Luke 23:34).

These verses are just a few of many Old Testament prophecies regarding the sacrificial death of the Messiah. Just as some do today, some in the days of the apostle Paul rejected the idea of a suffering Messiah. *"But we preach Christ crucified, unto the Jews a stumblingblock, and unto the Greeks foolishness: But unto them which are called, both Jews and Greeks, Christ the power of God, and the wisdom of God."* (I Corinthians 1:23-24). Their unbelief notwithstanding, the necessity of the sacrifice of Christ is clearly seen. *"But we see Jesus, who was made a little lower than the angels for the suffering of death, crowned with glory and honour; that he by the grace of God should taste death for every man."* (Hebrews 2:9). Sinful man cannot atone for his own sins. God's perfect justice (Deuteronomy 32:4) could only be satisfied by the sacrifice of the sinless Messiah (I Peter 2:21-24). *"Forasmuch as ye know that ye were not redeemed with corruptible things, as silver and gold, from your vain conversation received by tradition from your fathers; But with the precious blood of Christ, as of a lamb without blemish and without spot."* (I Peter 1:18-19). That sinless Messiah was God in the flesh (John 1:1,14), Jesus Christ.

Having devoted space to a discussion of the Messianic prophecies of Psalm 22 and their fulfillment in Jesus, we now give some time to an explanation of how this all serves as a source of comfort. There are two important points worthy of our consideration.

First, the agony experienced by the Messiah reminds us that our Lord is quite familiar with human suffering. He wept with the family of deceased Lazarus who mourned the loss of their loved one (John 11:35). He was saddened by the unfaithfulness of those whom He came to seek and to save (Luke 19:10,41). He was betrayed by a friend (Matthew 26:14-16). His closest confidants forsook Him in His hour of trial (Mark 14:50). As Isaiah prophesied of Him, Jesus was *"despised and rejected of men; a man of sorrows, and acquainted with grief..."* (Isaiah 53:3). When we say that the Lord understands our troubles, we genuinely and literally mean that He understands our troubles for He Himself met life's difficulties face to face as a man. As the apostle Paul wrote, *"Seeing then that we have a great high priest, that is passed into the heavens, Jesus the Son of God, let us hold fast our profession. For we have not an high priest which cannot be touched with the feeling of our infirmities; but was in all points tempted like as we are, yet without sin. Let us therefore come boldly unto the throne of grace, that we may obtain mercy, and find grace to help in time of need."* (Hebrews 4:14-16). No matter how deep the hurt in our hearts, in the Bible we have the words of the one who walked life's perilous path and in prayer we can go to the Father through Him (I Timothy 2:5).

Secondly, the suffering of the Savior reminds us to keep our earthly troubles in perspective. This life is not all there is. King Solomon wrote of man going *"to his long home."* (Ecclesiastes 12:5). Two verses later he said, *"Then shall the dust return to the earth as it was: and the spirit shall return unto God who gave it."* (Ecclesiastes 12:7). Regardless of the duration of any suffering we might experience, its length pales in comparison to eternity. We are all steadily marching toward the end of this life and the beginning of the next. Peter wrote, *"For all flesh is as grass, and all the glory of man as the flower of grass. The grass withereth, and the flower falleth away."* (I Peter 1:24). Hebrews 9:27 reads, *"And as it is appointed unto men once to die, but after this the judgment."* (Hebrews 9:27). This is a sobering thought and would indeed be most disturbing and depressing had it not been for that suffering Savior who paid the price for sin so that those who obey Him could face life's difficulties with the hope of heaven in their hearts. Because of the blood of Christ, a faithful Christian can look at life's challenges from the perspective of one who knows that these troubles are temporary rather than eternal. He or she can face troubles with assurance of eternal relief because Christ entered *"into heaven itself, now to appear in the presence of God for us."* (Hebrews 9:24).

Psalm 22 is indeed a remarkable reminder of the eternal comfort awaiting the faithful as a result of the suffering and ultimately victorious Messiah, Jesus Christ. *"And I heard a voice from heaven saying unto me, Write, Blessed are the dead which die in the Lord from henceforth: Yea, saith the Spirit, that they may rest from their labours: and their works do follow them."* (Revelation 14:13).

Chapter Five
Psalm 23
The Comfort of Realizing that the Shepherd Knows Me and I Know the Shepherd

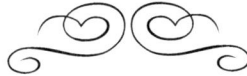

⧉

1The Lord is my shepherd; I shall not want.
2He maketh me to lie down in green pastures: he leadeth me beside the still waters.
3He restoreth my soul: he leadeth me in the paths of righteousness for his name's sake.
4Yea, though I walk through the valley of the shadow of death, I will fear no evil: for thou art with me; thy rod and thy staff they comfort me.
5Thou preparest a table before me in the presence of mine enemies: thou anointest my head with oil; my cup runneth over.
6Surely goodness and mercy shall follow me all the days of my life: and I will dwell in the house of the Lord for ever.

⧉

When it comes to providing comfort for the troubled soul, certainly no section of Sacred Scripture has been read more often than the twenty-third Psalm. The single sentence in verse four has no doubt consoled untold millions of breaking hearts as they watched the remains of their deceased loved ones being lowered into the earth or as they themselves confronted their own mortality. The very thought of having the Divine Shepherd lead His sheep into the unknown realms of eternity is enough to soothe the most troubled mind if we are following Him as our guide. Still, for all that this Psalm means to us as we contemplate death, its value as a source of comfort is much broader.

This Psalm is so rich and deep that entire books have been devoted to comments on it. There is no way that I can treat every precious facet of its meaning in just one chapter. That being the case, I want to focus on just one aspect of the Psalm, namely, the emphasis in the Psalm on the personal relationship between the Shepherd and the sheep.

Even a brief reading of the Psalm clearly shows that David, the inspired penman, is writing from the perspective of the sheep. Having once been a shepherd himself (I Samuel 16:11), he no doubt would have well understood the role of the shepherd and the needs of the sheep. Throughout the Psalm he uses the physical shepherd/sheep relationship to illustrate that which exists between God, the Divine Shepherd and those who faithfully follow Him through His Word.

The Psalmist inserts a personal pronoun into every verse. "*I shall not want…*" "*He maketh me to lie down…*" "*He restoreth my soul…*" In the King James Version there are 118 words in the Psalm. Of those, 17 are pronouns referring to the Psalmist himself. The Psalm opens and closes by identifying "the Lord" as the object of the inspired writer's affection. In between those verses, he repeatedly demonstrates that it is this Lord who is taking care of him, as 10 times he uses the pronouns "he," "his," "thy" and "thou." In essence, the great and mighty God, though He be the master of all creation (Genesis 1), still cares for His people individually and allows us to know Him on an intimate basis (I John 2:1-5). Any and every faithful child of God can say, "The Shepherd knows me and I know the Shepherd."

Suppose your favorite musician was performing in a huge outdoor stadium. Being such a loyal fan, you would be there with ticket in hand to join the tens of thousands of others who admire this talented individual. Now suppose that you've taken your seat among the screaming masses. The musician steps onto the stage and as he looks out over the packed stadium he spots you. He then promptly proceeds to the microphone and calls you by name to come down and see him. Can you begin to imagine how thrilled you would be? Here is this world-renowned musician singling you out by name in a crowd of upwards to a hundred thousand fans. It wouldn't even matter to you how he knew your name. Just knowing that he knew you and knowing that everyone in that stadium knew that he knew you would be incredible.

It's sad but true that what often excites us in the physical realm does nothing for us in the spiritual realm; yet to have the assurance that God as my Shepherd knows me personally is comfort beyond compare. As David brings out so beautifully in this Psalm, the Shepherd Divine doesn't just know about me. He knows ME and He knows my every need. It's because of this that "*I shall not want.*" I will never be in need of anything. My Shepherd knows what is best for me and He will readily provide all that I require. By giving concrete examples of the Shepherd's knowledge of and provision for the needs of His sheep, the next two verses expound on the fact that because "*the Lord is my Shepherd, I shall not want.*"

"*He maketh me to lie down in green pastures.*" God knows that we need emotional rest. He knows we need and want to be at peace. He also knows that the uncertainties of life can bring about worry and distress that can destroy inner peace. A sheep that is agitated by danger, disease, hunger or thirst will not lie down. Only in the abundance of pastures of tender grass will it feel content enough to not only lie down, but to rest comfortably. Through prayer, in which He allows us to cast our cares upon Him (I Peter 5:7) and through His written Word, by which our faith is established and strengthened (Romans 10:17), God has given us the green pastures in which we can relax and repose.

Notice just the words, "green pastures" in verse two. The shepherd will give his sheep a place to lie down. But where will it be? Will he lead them to dry, cracked, rock-covered clay much like what we see in the southern United States in the summer? No, he will lead them to the green pastures where his sheep can eat their fill and then lie down in the cool, soothing grass. He will give them his best. So it is with God the Shepherd. He offers us the best; the greenest of pastures, the highest of hopes, the pinnacle of peace, the zenith of comfort. No matter the level of our stresses, our hearts can be calm because our God knows our need for rest and peace and, what's more, He provides these blessings in abundance. Being plural, the word "pastures" suggests ongoing provision. Wherever there is a green pasture, the shepherd will take his sheep there. God doesn't offer us a crumb here and a morsel there. In Psalm 81:10 the Lord said, "*open thy mouth wide, and I will fill it.*" Psalm 23:5 speaks of the overflowing nature of God's blessings. Ephesians 3:20 reads, "*Now unto him that is able to do exceeding abundantly above all that we ask or think, according to the power that worketh in us."* We will never exhaust the blessings of God.

"He leadeth me beside the still waters." Now the sheep is thirsty. Does the shepherd lead it to the raging rapids and force it in? Of course not. He leads his sheep to "waters of quietness" as the alternate rendering of this phrase in the King James Version reads. If there is truth in the maxim that "still waters run deep," then we can see that this watering hole is not only a place of peacefulness, it is also a place of plenty as the water source is deep enough for the sheep to be able to drink its fill. As he has done in the first half of the verse, David is illustrating God's knowledge of the needs of His sheep and His abundant provision for same.

"He restoreth my soul" is a continuation of the thought presented in verse two. This is a beautiful statement that lends itself to the idea that he (the shepherd) brings the sheep back to life. The sheep is weary and thirsty due to its meandering. In providing for the needs of the sheep, the shepherd not only refreshes it, but also restores it. The word "restoreth" indicates continuous action. "He continually restores my soul." This is the case whenever we are distressed and seek God as the singular solution for our sadness. The world and its circumstances wear us down. We seek God through prayer and His written Word and every time we do He restores us. There is no limit to this. Just as the shepherd does not take a day off from giving his sheep the best, God's restoration is available 24 hours per day.

"He leadeth me in the paths of righteousness for his name's sake." God our Shepherd knows our spiritual needs as well as our physical. In Ezekiel 33:11 He said, *"I have no pleasure in the death of the wicked."* II Peter 3:9 says that God is *"not willing that any should perish, but that all should come to repentance."* Again picturing an earthly shepherd, we see him guiding his sheep along the safest path. Does that mean that there will not be any danger along the way? Certainly not, for the predators are lurking in the shadows, ready to attack. But the shepherd is there to guide and to guard. So it is with the Heavenly Shepherd. He wants His sheep to be with Him in eternity. He knows that along the path to the next world His sheep will face dangers as the *"adversary, the devil, as a roaring lion, walketh about, seeking whom he may devour."* (I Peter 5:8). Still, through the comfort of His Word (I Thessalonians 4:18) and the commands therein (John 14:15; 15:14; I John 5:3), He leads His sheep to the place of eternal rest.

Now the Psalmist turns from speaking about the Shepherd to speaking to the Shepherd and honoring Him for the tender care that was highlighted in the first three verses. Verses four through six express a calm assurance in God's guidance. There is not a "maybe" to be found here. The inspired writer has experienced the goodness of God and is confident that He will be with him throughout life and even into the valley of the shadow of death. He has found that the Lord was with him in good times and even in the bad when the enemy encompassed him. By his use of the continuous action verbs "preparest" and "anointest" in verse five, he shows that he is certain the Lord will continue to provide what he needs. In short, he knows this Shepherd and his knowledge of Him leads to the exultant conclusion in verse six, *"Surely goodness and mercy shall follow me all the days of my life: and I will dwell in the house of the Lord for ever."*

God blesses all of mankind. Jesus said, *"he maketh his sun to rise on the evil and on the good, and sendeth rain on the just and on the unjust."* (Matthew 5:45). Any and all blessings enjoyed by humanity come from God above (James 1:17). Unfortunately, not everyone in the world understands this. Many ignore the source of their blessings and thus, when trials come upon them, they think they have no one to whom they can turn. Faithful children of God on the other hand know the source of their blessings. They regularly acknowledge God's provision in their daily service to Him. When they face life's trials, they know where to turn for comfort because they have learned to rely on and trust in God. They know that the one who has sustained them in life's noonday will carry them through the darkest midnight. Like the sheep portrayed in this Psalm, they have seen that the goodness of God endures continually (Psalm 52:1). They know the Shepherd and confidently look ahead, assured that this Shepherd will be there for them.

The Shepherd knows me and I know the Shepherd. These two facts that are clearly demonstrated in the twenty-third Psalm combine to comfort our souls at a depth that no worldly thought could ever fathom. God knows me whether or not I acknowledge Him (Romans 3:3-4), but when I realize through faith that God knows me so well that He can understand my every need and thus provide what is best for me in whatever situation I may find myself as a faithful Christian, then I can rejoice with the author of this Psalm and confidently apply his Divinely inspired words to my own life no matter how dark or discouraging my way might become.

Chapter Six
Psalm 29
The Comfort of Knowing That God Is In Control

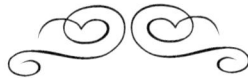

₁Give unto the Lord, O ye mighty, give unto the Lord glory and strength.

₂Give unto the Lord the glory due unto his name; worship the Lord in the beauty of holiness.

₃The voice of the Lord is upon the waters: the God of glory thundereth: the Lord is upon many waters.

₄The voice of the Lord is powerful; the voice of the Lord is full of majesty.

₅The voice of the Lord breaketh the cedars; yea, the Lord breaketh the cedars of Lebanon.

₆He maketh them also to skip like a calf; Lebanon and Sirion like a young unicorn.

₇The voice of the Lord divideth the flames of fire.

₈The voice of the Lord shaketh the wilderness; the Lord shaketh the wilderness of Kadesh.

₉The voice of the Lord maketh the hinds to calve, and discovereth the forests: and in his temple doth every one speak of his glory.

₁₀The Lord sitteth upon the flood; yea, the Lord sitteth King for ever.

₁₁The Lord will give strength unto his people; the Lord will bless his people with peace.

Even before looking at this Psalm's context and original meaning to its readers, one fact jumps off the page. God is in control. Just a quick reading of Psalm 29 must cause one to stop and say in prayer to our Lord, "How great thou art!" He is in control of earth. He is in control of eternity. All of His creation bows down before His might. What a powerful God we serve.

One might wonder, "If God is in control, why is there so much suffering in the world? Why doesn't God do something about it?" The answer lies in the fact that God has given mankind freedom of choice. Now, that may sound like a simplistic solution to some but it's true. In the Garden of Eden, the first man and woman were given the freedom to choose to obey or not to obey God. In making the wrong choice, they introduced sin into the world (Genesis 3). That creation that had been "very good" (Genesis 1:31) had been corrupted. Now it was subject to wearing down (Psalm 102:25-26). Aging, decay and ultimately death would now result. The imperfections in the world are the result of mankind's fall, not God's lack of power, and we suffer as a result of these imperfections.

On a more personal note, sometimes we suffer as individuals because of poor choices that we make. Our health, our financial situation, our relationships may cause us pain because we have exercised our freedom of choice and have done the wrong things. The apostle Paul wrote, "*Some men's sins are open beforehand, going before to judgment; and some men they follow after.*" (I Timothy 5:24).

Sometimes we suffer as individuals because of poor choices that others make. We may suffer from an accident caused by a drunk driver, go through financial difficulties because the company for which we worked closed due to the dishonesty of the owner or even feel grief over losing a loved one who himself made a poor choice.

Again, although the fact that freedom of choice explains the existence of suffering in the world, some don't want to accept this. They think that God has abandoned them in their sorrow. If they will think about it, they have put themselves in a difficult position. They want their freedom to do as they please, but then they want God to take away that freedom and intervene so that they won't have to suffer any pain. When Job was encouraged by his wife to curse God and die due to his affliction, he replied, "*What? Shall we receive good at the hand of God, and shall we not receive evil?*" (Job 2:10). Of course, Job was not charging God with committing wickedness for there is no evil in God (James 1:13). What he was saying is that it's inconsistent to follow God when things are going well and turn on Him when times get tough. We appreciate the freedom that God has given us when it brings blessings, but do we complain when this same freedom brings difficulties?

Acceptance of the fact that we live in a sinful, imperfect world where tragedies occur and bad things happen to good people is certainly one of the key results of faith. Psalm 29 is so powerful because, coming from the source of our faith (Romans 10:17), it reminds us that no matter how difficult our situation might be, God is aware and in control of that situation.

Reminding us that God is in control, our faith looks beyond this world and its imperfection and into eternity where heaven awaits with its absence of tears, death, sorrow and pain (Revelation 21:4). Paul painted this beautiful contrast in I Corinthians 15:21-22: "*For since by man came death, by man came also the resurrection of the dead. For as in Adam all die, even so in Christ shall all be made alive.*"

Yes, God is in control. He is not controlling in the sense that He dangles us from a string as a puppeteer does his puppets. He is not dominating our every move, restraining or permitting our actions as though we had no minds of our own. He is in control in the sense that He knows what's going on. He sees us. Best of all, He has made provision for us to be in a better land than this through obedience to the Gospel that He established through Jesus Christ. He was in control of that opportunity for salvation at least as far back as the Garden of Eden right after the man and woman wrongly exercised their freedom of choice and sinned (Genesis 3:15).

God is in control. We can look all about us and see the evidence as the Psalmist did. This is especially significant when we face difficulties and feel that our lives are out of control. The truth is, there are indeed times when we cannot be in control. Sometimes there is only so much that we can do to affect our situation. It's unfortunate that it can take times like this to drive us to our knees and turn to the one who is in control but then again, these times of trial can actually benefit us by preparing us for greater service here and eternal rest after this life is over.

In the midst of life's challenges, we must listen to the "voice of the Lord." No, we're not to sit around and wait for the Lord to audibly address us. The voice of the Lord in Psalm 29 was not the literal voice of God. The writer used the term to represent the power and omnipresence of God. Carefully read through the Psalm again, recognizing the greatness of our God and then pause to realize that this God knows of the difficulties that we face when we are in the very midst of them and that He will care for us. He is in the midst of these situations with us. "*The Lord will give strength unto his people; the Lord will bless his people with peace.*" He has it all under control.

Chapter Seven
Psalm 34
The Comfort of God-fearing Fearlessness

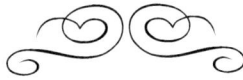

1I will bless the Lord at all times: his praise shall continually be in my mouth.

2My soul shall make her boast in the Lord: the humble shall hear thereof, and be glad.

3O magnify the Lord with me, and let us exalt his name together.

4I sought the Lord and he heard me, and delivered me from all my fears.

5They looked unto him, and were lightened: and their faces were not ashamed.

6This poor man cried, and the Lord heard him, and saved him out of all his troubles.

7The angel of the Lord encampeth round about them that fear him, and delivereth them.

8O taste and see that the Lord is good: blessed is the man that trusteth in him.

9O fear the Lord, ye his saints: for there is no want to them that fear him.

10The young lions do lack, and suffer hunger: but they that seek the Lord shall not want any good thing.

11Come, ye children, hearken unto me: I will teach you the fear of the Lord.

12What man is he that desireth life, and loveth many good days, that he may see good?

13Keep thy tongue from evil, and thy lips from speaking guile.

14Depart from evil, and do good; seek peace, and pursue it.

15The eyes of the Lord are upon the righteous, and his ears are open unto their cry.

16The face of the Lord is against them that do evil, to cut off the remembrance of them from the earth.

17The righteous cry, and the Lord heareth, and delivereth them out of all their troubles.

18The Lord is nigh unto them that are of a broken heart; and saveth such as be of a contrite spirit.

19Many are the afflictions of the righteous: but the Lord delivereth him out of them all.

20He keepeth all his bones: not one of them is broken.

21Evil shall slay the wicked: and they that hate the righteous shall be desolate.

22The Lord redeemeth the soul of his servants: and none of them that trust in him shall be desolate.

At first glance the title of this chapter appears to be a contradiction in terms. How could one fear and yet be fearless? The answer is found in the type of fear that one should have, namely, fear of God. This fear is enjoined in verse 9. One of its benefits is found in the same verse. That it is something that can be taught is seen in verse 11 and actions that proceed from it are demonstrated in verses 12 through 14.

In essence, to fear God is to revere, respect and honor God and be in awe of Him. This fear is cited in other Bible passages. Solomon wrote that "*the fear of the Lord is the beginning of knowledge…*" (Proverbs 1:7). Later he said, "*The fear of the Lord is the beginning of wisdom: and the knowledge of the holy is understanding.*" (Proverbs 9:10). The Psalmist said, "*The fear of the Lord is clean, enduring for ever…*" (Psalm 19:9).

With the fear of the Lord in one's heart, he or she will submit themselves to the will of the Lord. They will strive to lead lives of purity. Again, refer to verses 12 through 14. In addition, consider Solomon's words in Proverbs 16:6. *"By mercy and truth iniquity is purged: and by the fear of the Lord men depart from evil."* This fear leads one to faithful obedience to God which in turn leads to the blessings mentioned in this Psalm. These blessings include deliverance (verses 6-7 and 19), abundance (verse 10), God's ear in prayer (verse 15), God's constant presence (verse 18) and God's continual care (verse 22), each of which provides comfort.

When one has the fear of the Lord in his heart, he blesses God, praises God, magnifies God and exalts God by his humble obedience. When he does this, thus surrendering to the Lord, he is able to take whatever troubles him, including his fears, and turn everything over to God (verse 4).

If you have ever had any difficulties then you know from experience that walking hand in hand with that trouble, maybe even leading the way for it, is the feeling of fear. When financial challenges come, fear of loss, fear of failure and fear of embarrassment or shame rise up and show their ugly faces. When illness invades our lives, fear of pain, fear of financial distress and even fear of death make themselves known. When a loved one dies, fear of loneliness can creep in. Every one of these fears is potentially crippling to one's emotional state, one's physical condition and one's spirituality. The fear of God that recognizes the power of the Almighty to relieve these fears is the only way to defeat them.

It's terrible to be afraid, but when we break down fear we find that it is typically the result of a lack of knowledge. We're facing trouble and we don't know how it will all turn out. As a result, we're afraid. We've seen horrible things happen to others in our situation and we assume that our situation is going to turn out the same way. This family lost their house. That person suffered a lot of pain and spent weeks in the hospital. Often we've made up our minds that our results will be the same or even worse. Adding to this are the "friends" who seem to take delight in sharing their horror stories with us.

This lack of knowledge which breeds fear can easily be replaced with that which conquers fear. God has given us His inspired Word to fill that knowledge gap and allows us to come and speak to Him in prayer to cast these fears upon Him. Thus, faith replaces fear. There is not enough room in the human heart for both.

In order to gain freedom from fear, we first have to acknowledge its presence and then identify it. The Psalmist acknowledged his fears in prayer. *"I sought the Lord…"* (verse 3). *"This poor man cried…"* (verse 6). To acknowledge fear is to admit that it's there. Why would we not tell this to God? He already knows our hearts (I Chronicles 28:9). Why would we deny the existence of our fears in His presence?

Identifying fear is just as important as acknowledging it. Playing out scenarios, both positive and negative, can be helpful. During the illness of my wife, Shannon, she and I discussed our fears in the early days of her disease. We would ask, "What is making you afraid and why does that scare you?" We shared a fear of the unknown. She feared the cancer treatments, the sickness that might come with them, the loss of hair and the loss of strength. My fears included those of not being able to adequately take care of her and, of course, that of losing her. As we examined each fear we kept coming back to one conclusion. Whatever we didn't know about what would happen, we were certain that God knew. Whatever fears we entertained were eliminated by such powerful statements as, *"I can do all things through Christ which strengtheneth me."* (Philippians 4:13). That's how we made it through that particular trial of life. She showed such tremendous courage throughout her ordeal and even in death she refused to allow fear to discourage her. Faith, grounded firmly in fear of the Lord, produced fearlessness that allowed her to overcome.

When troubles come, ask yourself or discuss with someone else what is making you afraid. Spend time in prayer to God and tell Him what is making you afraid. Verse 18 of this Psalm says that the Lord is near. II Timothy 1:7 says, *"For God hath not given us the spirit of fear; but of power, and of love, and of a sound mind."* The word "fear" in this passage means "timidity, fearfulness, cowardice." I John 4:18 reads, *"There is no fear in love; but perfect love casteth out fear: because fear hath torment. He that feareth is not made perfect in love."* The word for "fear" in this verse means "dread, terror." Face the troubling fears and then turn in reverential fear to the one who can deliver you from them.

Chapter Eight
Psalm 73
The Comfort of God's Patience

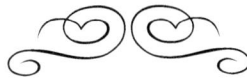

1Truly, God is good to Israel, even to such as are of a clean heart.

2But as for me, my feet were almost gone; my steps had well nigh slipped.

3For I was envious at the foolish, when I saw the prosperity of the wicked.

4For there are no bands in their death: but their strength is firm.

5They are not in trouble as other men; neither are they plagued like other men.

6Therefore pride compasseth them about as a chain; violence covereth them as a garment.

7Their eyes stand out with fatness: they have more than heart could wish.

8They are corrupt, and speak wickedly against oppression: they speak loftily.

9They set their mouth against the heavens, and their tongue walketh through the earth.

10Therefore his people return hither: and waters of a full cup are wrung out to them.

11And they say, How doth God know? and is there knowledge in the most High?

12Behold, these are the ungodly, who prosper in the world; they increase in riches.

13Verily I have cleansed my heart in vain, and washed my hands in innocency.

14For all the day long have I been plagued, and chastened every morning.

15If I say, I will speak thus; behold, I should offend against the generation of thy children.

16When I thought to know this, it was too painful for me;

17Until I went into the sanctuary of God; then understood I their end.

18Surely thou didst set them in slippery places: thou castedst them down into destruction.

19How are they brought into desolation, as in a moment! they are utterly consumed with terrors.

20As a dream when one awaketh; so, O Lord, when thou awakest, thou shalt despise their image.

21Thus my heart was grieved, and I was pricked in my reins.

22So foolish was I, and ignorant: I was as a beast before thee.

23Nevertheless I am continually with thee: thou hast holden me by my right hand.

24Thou shalt guide me with thy counsel, and afterward receive me to glory.

25Whom have I in heaven but thee? and there is none upon earth that I desire beside thee.

26My flesh and my heart faileth: but God is the strength of my heart, and my portion for ever.

27For, lo, they that are far from thee shall perish: thou hast destroyed all them that go a whoring from thee.

28But it is good for me to draw near to God: I have put my trust in the Lord God, that I may declare all thy works.

This Psalm is unique in that the writer states his conclusion in his introduction. He had come to the conclusion that God is good to those of a clean heart. He does recall a time, however, in which he had forgotten this fact. We could aptly title verses two through fourteen, "Where Was God?" for the writer's words describe a period in his life when he felt that God had withdrawn Himself from the world and forsaken His people.

As has typically been the case throughout history, the society in which this writer lived was dominated by wickedness. The evil of those surrounding the Psalmist was compounded by their attitude that either God didn't know about their sinfulness or else didn't care. Their arrogance influenced the Psalmist to question his own service to God. *"Verily I have cleansed my heart in vain, and washed my hands in innocency."* Surely faithfulness was a waste of time. Either God was too weak to act or just wholly unconcerned about both the wicked and the righteous. This is the frame of mind in which the writer found himself. As he had said in verse 2, *"But as for me, my feet were almost gone; my steps had well nigh slipped."*

When the Psalmist turned his attention from the world and turned his eyes toward God, he saw the truth. He saw that while the wicked may prosper in this life, they will be cast down in eternity. He saw how the scales may appear to be tipped toward a life of disobedience while on earth but then realized that the rewards of eternity are far greater than anything this world might have to offer. He repented. He turned back to God. He expressed shame for his foolishness and ignorance.

What does the Psalmist's situation have to do with finding comfort when we're facing life's troubles? Very simply, he wondered about God's care just like we might do in our struggles and grief. "Where was God?" is a typical question on the hearts if not on the lips of those who suffer. "Where was God when my spouse died?" "Where was God when my child was maimed in a car wreck?" "Where was God (fill in the blank)?" The temptation is to conclude that either He doesn't care or, if He does care, perhaps He is just too weak to do anything to help. Perhaps there is no hope. Perhaps we've either been abandoned or the one in whom we have put so much trust just can't deliver on the promises that He has made.

Other chapters in this book deal with how to overcome this doubt. Suffice it to say here that it can be overcome. This chapter is about an underlying theme of Psalm 73. The writer wondered. He questioned. He doubted. In spite of all of this, God was patient with him. The Psalmist wasn't struck dead after writing the last letter of verse 14. God was patient with him.

Wondering about God's care is not uncommon in the Psalms. Psalm 10:1 reads, *"Why standest afar off, O Lord? why hidest thou thyself in times of trouble."* Psalm 74 begins, *"O God, why hast thou cast us off for ever? why doth thine anger smoke against the sheep of thy pasture?"* Psalm 79 opens with the writer describing the affliction that Jerusalem was experiencing at the hands of the heathen. He could not understand why God had not yet intervened (Psalm 79:5). Certainly we can feel the frustration of these writers. Perhaps we can even sense an aggravation with God's timing. These writers are neither the first nor the last to want things to happen on their schedule rather than on God's. In spite of their bewilderment and outright questioning of the Lord's ways, they were treated with patience by the benevolent God who created them.

It's interesting to listen to people's observations about incidents recorded in the Bible. Some will read the complaints of Israel in the wilderness after they were freed from Egyptian captivity (Exodus 15ff) and sneer, figuring that these people should have known better. Some will look at the often seen faithlessness of even the apostles as they walked with Jesus when He was in the flesh and smugly shake their heads in disgust over the weakness of those men who had been hand-picked by Jesus. Thankfully, none of us has been charged with filling God's role. While we might look down our noses at the recorded demonstrations of weak faith, God, who was there when each event occurred, showed patience and allowed for growth, just like He does when we demonstrate weakness in our faith.

One word that is used in the King James translation to express God's patience is "longsuffering." In the Old Testament the word can be found in Exodus 34:6, Numbers 14:18, Psalm 86:15 and Jeremiah 15:15. New Testament usages as the word regards God's longsuffering toward mankind include Romans 9:22, I Timothy 1:16, I Peter 3:20, II Peter 3:9 and II Peter 3:15. The Greek word that is used in the New Testament passages is a compound word. The first half is the word from which we derive our English word, "macro," meaning large in scale, scope or capability. The second half has to do with heat, anger or passion. In the compound word translated "longsuffering," we see our God as one who is great in withholding His anger. He does not respond in the heat of a moment. As Peter wrote in II Peter 3:9, *"The Lord is not slack concerning his promise, as some men count slackness; but is longsuffering to us-ward, not willing that any should perish, but that all should come to repentance."* Regarding God's response to Israel's complaints and unfaithfulness in the wilderness the Psalmist wrote, *"But he, being full of compassion, forgave their iniquity, and destroyed them not: yea, many a time turned he his anger away, and did not stir up all his wrath. For he remembered that they were but flesh; a wind that passeth away, and cometh not again."* (Psalm 78:38-39). In the throes of Judah's sorrows, Jeremiah wrote, *"It is of the Lord's mercies that we are not consumed, because his compassions fail not. They are new every morning: great is thy faithfulness."* (Lamentations 3:22-23). God is patient with the frailties of His creation.

As was mentioned in another chapter, when dealing with life's challenges, we typically talk about the need for time to work through them. It's because our situation is so new, so unfamiliar that we need some time to adjust. In the death of a loved one, for instance, that first night of not having him or her around or that first time that you want to talk to him or her but cannot are scenarios that require adjustment. We have to get used to this uncharted territory in our lives. Some choose to get angry over these unwanted and sometimes unexpected changes. Some question God's goodness and even challenge Him. Thanks be to God that He knows the hearts of those who feel these very real, very human emotional pangs.

Of the many wonderful attributes of our God, one is that He never turns His ear from any of the prayers of the righteous (I John 5:14-15). We are invited to cast our cares (anxieties) upon Him (I Peter 5:7). We can tell Him anything, expressing the deepest feelings from the most remote chambers of our hearts. We can speak to God openly like Habakkuk did in his dilemma (Habakkuk 1:2ff). We can tell Him of our confusion regarding our situation as the writer of Psalm 73 did. Our God understands and we go to Him through our mediator, Jesus Christ (I Timothy 2:5) who Himself walked in our shoes, as it were, and *"was in all points tempted like as we are…"* (Hebrews 4:15). In fact, because of Christ, we can *"come boldly unto the throne of grace, that we may obtain mercy, and find grace to help in time of need."* (Hebrews 4:16). God allows us and even encourages us to pour out our hearts to Him. "Trust in him at all times; ye people, pour out your heart before him: God is a refuge for us." (Psalm 62:8). He listens patiently, making allowance for our human imperfection. *"Like as a father pitieth his children, so the Lord pitieth them that fear him. For he knoweth our frame; he remembereth that we are dust."* (Psalm 103:13-14).

The Lord inspired the writer of Psalm 73 to put down in words the feelings that had filled his heart in a desperate period of his life. In so doing, God showed that He appreciates His people's lack of understanding and even doubt when we are afflicted. Of course, it should be pointed out that God's patience can be exhausted. While He showed an incredible measure of longsuffering to Israel in the wilderness, eventually He wearied of the rebellious attitudes and refused many of the Israelites entrance into the promised land of Canaan

(Numbers 14). The apostle Paul wrote that God "*hath appointed a day, in the which he will judge the world in righteousness by that man whom he hath ordained...*" (Acts 17:31). He also wrote that the Lord will exact punishment against those who "*know not God, and that obey not the gospel of our Lord Jesus Christ.*" (II Thessalonians 1:7-9). Even Christians can go too far away from God and lose their souls (II Peter 2:20-22). We must not allow our questioning to turn into disbelief. Instead, we must imitate this Psalmist. Even though at one point he wondered about God's care for him, he nonetheless relied on the faith that he had built through God's Word and ultimately concluded that God is good. If we do like him, we will see that God is caring for us as much in our challenges as He does in our times of peace. May we say with Habakkuk, "*Although the fig tree shall not blossom, neither shall fruit be in the vines; the labour of the olive shall fail, and the fields shall yield no meat; the flock shall be cut off from the fold, and there shall be no herd in the stalls: Yet will I rejoice in the Lord, I will joy in the God of my salvation.*" (Habakkuk 3:17-18). Let us be thankful that we serve the God who makes a way for us to escape our troubles (I Corinthians 10:13) and who patiently allows us time to work through them.

Chapter Nine
Psalm 77
The Comfort of Remembering

1I cried unto God with my voice, even unto God with my voice; and he gave ear unto me.
2In the day of my trouble I sought the Lord: my sore ran in the night, and ceased not: my soul refused to be comforted.
3I remembered God, and was troubled: I complained, and my spirit was overwhelmed. Selah.
4Thou holdest mine eyes waking: I am so troubled that I cannot speak.
5I have considered the days of old, the years of ancient times.
6I will call to remembrance my song in the night: I commune with mine own heart: and my spirit made diligent search.
7Will the Lord cast off for ever? and will he be favourable no more?
8Is his mercy clean gone for ever? doth his promise fail for evermore?
9Hath God forgotten to be gracious? hath he in anger shut up his tender mercies? Selah.
10And I said, This is my infirmity: but I will remember the years of the right hand of the most High.
11I will remember the works of the Lord: surely I will

remember thy wonders of old.
12I will meditate also of all thy work, and talk of thy doings.
13Thy way, O God, is in the sanctuary: who is so great a
God as our God?
14Thou art the God that doest wonders: thou hast declared
thy strength among the people.
15Thou hast with thine arm redeemed thy people, the sons of
Jacob and Joseph. Selah.
16The waters saw thee, O God, the waters saw thee; they were
afraid: the depths also were troubled.
17The clouds poured out water: the skies sent out a sound:
thine arrows also went abroad.
18The voice of thy thunder was in the heaven: the lightnings
lightened the world: the earth trembled and shook.
19Thy way is in the sea, and thy path in the great waters, and
thy footsteps are not known.
20Thou leddest thy people like a flock by the hand of Moses
and Aaron.

The agony being suffered by this Psalmist is clearly seen in the first four verses. His sorrow was so deep that silent prayer was not sufficient to utter it. He audibly cried out to God, even through the night. The overwhelming nature of his sadness had robbed him of sleep. It was an anguish that knew no depths, as it spiraled downward from that which could only be expressed out loud to that which was so intense that no words could even come forth from the Psalmist's lips to articulate it.

The setting of this Psalm is open to discussion. It appears to be a captivity Psalm, one written after the citizens of Judah were taken away from their home country into servitude in the land of the Babylonians (II Chronicles 36:14-21). In verses seven through nine, the writer is obviously lamenting a tragic loss. In the final eleven verses, he is bringing to mind a previous deliverance that his ancestors had enjoyed – the deliverance of Israel from Egyptian bondage (Exodus 12-14). In remembering how God had freed Israel from slavery in the past, perhaps the Psalmist is expressing that same hope of God's deliverance of Judah from their present distress.

Look at the contrast of thought in verses one through nine. Initially, the Psalmist writes of how he turned to God in his sorrow, but then he wonders where God is and why He will not answer his earlier pleas. *"I begged for relief to the extent that I had no more words to speak. Why has God not answered me? Has He forgotten how to be gracious?"* Questioning if God had forgotten is ironic because it is actually the Psalmist himself who had forgotten something. He had forgotten the history of God's goodness toward His people. Notice how his attitude changes when he says in verse 11, *"I will remember the works of the Lord: surely I will remember thy wonders of old."* From that point on he recounts how God had released Israel from the life-stealing grip of the Egyptians and in the midst of this he exclaims, *"Who is so great a God as our God?"* (verse 13).

This apparent conflict in the heart of the Psalmist is not at all unfamiliar to anyone who has ever been in sorrow. We pray and plead, hoping, perhaps even expecting, that God will answer our prayers our way in our time. If He does not, we may begin to question His goodness. We may feel that the distress will never go away. We forget that God has not changed and perhaps we even forget all the good that we have enjoyed in life at His hand of mercy.

With so many emotions flying around in our heads during times of trouble, it's easy to see how remembrances of God's goodness could be crowded out. That's why it is critical for the sake of our souls for us to stop, take some time for ourselves and remember. That's what the Psalmist did. Look at verses 12 and 13. In his despair, he put a halt to the doubts he was having long enough to take time to focus on God. He meditated on His works, talked of His doings and considered His way. In so doing, he recalled that the Lord is *the God that doest wonders"* (verse 14). Going back to Israel's deliverance from Egypt, the Psalmist concludes that the God who did that could certainly answer his pleas and provide the comfort he was so desperately seeking.

Simply telling someone in sorrow to "remember God" may seem trite and may even be met with anger by the one who is suffering. Some may think I'm being simplistic and even trivializing one's sadness by saying, "Remember God." It may sound like I'm impatiently telling the sorrowful, "Come on; snap out of it. Stop moping around and get over it." Nothing could be further from the truth.

When a loved one dies, what is one of the first things done by those left behind? Certainly we cry and hurt and maybe even question, but do we not also remember? Most likely we find ourselves sitting around a dinner table with family and friends sharing pleasant memories of the deceased. There is great comfort in this. As weeks, months and years pass, we will still with startling regularity remember different things about our beloved. Memories might be triggered by a scent, a picture, a song or even a phrase. One of the statements my wife, Shannon made before she died was, "This is it." I can still see the calm, fearless look in her face and hear the genuine anticipation in her voice as she said that. Since that time, whenever I have heard that three word phrase I have thought of her. I'm sure this memory will never leave me.

If remembering moments in the life of our departed loved one can cheer us and bring us comfort, why would not remembering God's goodness bring us even greater joy and peace? If we can sit around and begin conversations with, "Remember when he (or she) did this or that" and not get angry or take offense, then why can we not just as well begin conversations with, "Remember when God said this in His Word?" or "Remember when God blessed you with…"? A memory is a valuable tool in so many ways, not the least of which is in bringing to mind the multiplicity of demonstrations of God's goodness both as recorded in His Word and as experienced in our lives.

In the situation in which this Psalmist found himself, remembering Israel's release from Egypt was the most comforting. He knew from that historical event that God both could and would do whatever was necessary to aid His people. The amazing power of God is so beautifully portrayed in the Psalmist's statement about the parting of the Red Sea in verse 16. "*The waters saw thee, O God, the waters saw thee; they were afraid: the depths also were troubled.*" In verses 18 through 20 he declares that God was to be found everywhere in this scene of deliverance. He was in the thunder and lightning and the quaking of the earth. He was in the midst of the sea. Yet for all of the demonstration of His might, God carefully led each Israelite through the sea like a shepherd leads his flock. From distress to doubt to adulation, the Psalmist runs the gamut of emotions, concluding the Psalm with his remembrance of God's goodness.

In whatever situation we may be, we can remember how God blessed His faithful followers in life's daylight and how He led them through life's midnight as well as how He promises to do the same for us if we are faithful Christians. When in financial straits, we can go to Matthew 6:25-34 and remember our value in the eyes of God as well as His promise, "*But seek ye first the kingdom of God, and his righteousness; and all these things shall be added unto you.*" (Matthew 6:33). When grieving, we can go to the eleventh chapter of John and remember the compassion of Jesus as He wept with the family and friends of

Lazarus (John 11:35). When lonely, we can consult Hebrews 13:5-6 in which Paul wrote, "*Let your conversation be without covetousness; and be content with such things as ye have: for he hath said, I will never leave thee, nor forsake thee. So that we may boldly say, The Lord is my helper, and I will not fear what man shall do unto me.*" When we feel like giving up, we can turn to Romans 8 and remember Paul's inspired words regarding hope, God's providential care and the Lord's amazing love. When it seems that the pull of the world is too strong, we can go to I John 4:4 and remember the words of the apostle John: "*Ye are of God, little children, and have overcome them: because greater is he that is in you, than he that is in the world.*" When we ourselves are facing death, we can read the fifteenth chapter of First Corinthians regarding the resurrection unto eternal life, especially the final five verses.

> So when this corruptible shall have put on incorruption, and this mortal shall have put on immortality, then shall be brought to pass the saying that is written, Death is swallowed up in victory. O death, where is thy sting? O grave, where is thy victory? The sting of death is sin; and the strength of sin is the law. But thanks be to God, which giveth us the victory through our Lord Jesus Christ. Therefore, my beloved brethren, be ye stedfast, unmoveable, always abounding in the work of the Lord, forasmuch as ye know that your labour is not in vain in the Lord.

Not only can we remember the inspired records of God's help and His promises, we can also recall in our own lives how greatly God has always blessed us. In the midst of our troubles, the sorrow is deeply rooted in our hearts. It certainly will not subside over night and may linger for days or weeks on end. In this context, about all we can see and feel is our sorrow and its cause. It takes effort, sometimes considerable effort, but there are fond remembrances of God's goodness within us just waiting to come forth and bring us comfort. Remembering these things does not diminish the depth of the sadness, but it can cause us to stop and realize how great God has been to us through the years. In fact, it could remind that even in our despair, God is still as close as He has ever been. To live in the past is unproductive, but to visit it from time to time through remembering the marvelous blessings of God can make our present more bearable and our future brighter. "*Rejoice in the Lord, ye righteous; and give thanks at the remembrance of his holiness.*" (Psalm 97:12).

Chapter Ten
Psalm 84
Comfort "At the End of the Day"

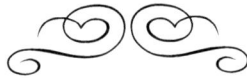

1How amiable are thy tabernacles, O Lord of hosts!
2My soul longeth, yea, even fainteth for the courts of the
Lord: my heart and my flesh crieth out for the living God.
3Yea, the sparrow hath found an house, and the swallow a
nest for herself, where she may lay her young, even thine
altars, O Lord of hosts, my King, and my God.
4Blessed are they that dwell in thy house: they will be still
praising thee. Selah.
5Blessed is the man whose strength is in thee; in whose hearts
are the ways of them.
6Who passing through the valley of Baca make it a well; the
rain also filleth the pools.
7They go from strength to strength, every one of them in
Zion appeareth before God.
8O Lord God of hosts, hear my prayer: give ear, O God of
Jacob. Selah.
9Behold, O God our shield, and look upon the face of thine
anointed.
10For a day in thy courts is better than a thousand. I had
rather be a doorkeeper in the house of my God, than to dwell

in the tents of wickedness.
11For the Lord God is a sun and shield: the Lord will give
grace and glory: no good thing will he withhold from them
that walk uprightly.
12O Lord of hosts, blessed is the man that trusteth in thee.

People like to use the phrase, "at the end of the day." For example, a nurse might say something like, "Well, yes, the work I do is difficult but at the end of the day it's a good feeling to know that I've been able to help someone." When one uses this phrase he or she is saying that in spite of any apparent drawbacks to their situation or any apparent positives of someone else's situation, they're still thankful to be who they are and where they are.

The phrase brings to mind the story of the cross-bearing man who walked into the "cross store." He laid down his cross and said to the proprietor, "I want a lighter cross please; one that's easier to carry." The proprietor invited him to look around the store. The shopper went from one cross to another, examining each carefully. He tried to lift one but was barely able to budge it. Just glancing at another he knew that he could never handle it. One by one he eliminated those that he figured would be too burdensome. Finally he came to one that looked manageable. He picked it up and marveled at how light it was. "I'll take this one," the man said. "That one, sir," answered the proprietor, "is the one you carried in here." So often we think our lot in life is worse than anyone else's, only to discover "at the end of the day" that it's not so unbearable after all.

At the end of the day, this Psalmist was a child of God. Whatever else the world had to offer, whatever challenges life presented, he declared that he would rather be the lowliest servant waiting on others at the door of God's house than to have a fine existence away from the Lord and in service to Satan.

The entire Psalm paints a beautiful picture of how wonderful it is to be a child of God. The word "amiable" in the opening verse means lovely or beloved. There is great joy in serving God (verse 3). Blessings and happiness follow those who abide in the Lord (verses 4-5). The reason for this happiness is because of God who alone is the sun and shield, the source of grace and glory, the giver of bountiful blessings (verse 11).

What troubles are we facing in our lives? Are we grieving the loss of a loved one? Are we enduring physical illness in our lives or in the life of someone we love? Are we wrestling with financial insecurity and/or job loss? Do family troubles burden us? Is it possible that those who don't obey God are free from these troubles? Would we be better off to give up on God and just fall in with the world so that our problems will go away? The answer is a resounding "NO." Those who live in disobedience to God have troubles too. They get sick, lose loved ones, have personal struggles just like faithful Christians do. BUT AT THE END OF THE DAY it's the Christian who has the Lord as his or her sun and shield, it's the Christian who has an eternal shoulder on which to lean and a loving ear ready to hear (I Peter 5:7; Revelation 5:8) and it's the Christian who has hope of eternal rest when this life is over (Romans 8:24-25).

"A day in thy courts is better than a thousand." Just one day following God is better than a thousand following Satan. This single day, though it be filled with the world's snares is worth more than a thousand days of temporal pleasure lived in service to the king of the damned. If one day in God's service is worth this much, a lifetime of faithfulness to Him has value beyond compare.

Satan delights in seeing trouble come upon the human race. His ultimate desire is to have as many as he can with him in eternal hell (I Peter 5:8). To him, troubles serve as a way to retrieve those who left him and turned to God and a way to hang on to those who are currently serving him.

Psalm 84 shows us that Satan really has nothing worthwhile to offer us. When we face difficulties and turn our backs on God, we turn to one who is inferior to God in every way and, at best, offers us only temporary relief, if it can even be called relief. The "relief" that an ungodly life offers to our difficulties is found in drugs, indecent living, anger and bitterness. On the other hand, when our hearts and flesh cry out for the living God (verse 2), we find blessings, grace and peace, as well as the strength we need to endure (verses 4-5).

It may seem sometimes that we are fighting a losing battle, that the hurt that befalls us is too great to bear and that it's just not worth the daily effort to follow God faithfully. This Psalm proves otherwise. People of the world may boast of their lives, but at the end of the day, it is the faithful child of God who has the comfort and strength that he or she needs to handle life's issues. Following God faithfully, even in the midst of struggles, is never a mistake, but is always rewarding.

Chapter Eleven
Psalm 91
Comfort In Knowing That Nothing Can Really Harm Us

1He that dwelleth in the secret place of the most High shall abide under the shadow of the Almighty.

2I will say of the Lord, He is my refuge and my fortress: my God; in him will I trust.

3Surely he shall deliver thee from the snare of the fowler, and from the noisome pestilence.

4He shall cover thee with his feathers, and under his wings shalt thou trust: his truth shall be thy shield and buckler.

5Thou shalt not be afraid for the terror by night; nor for the arrow that flieth by day;

6Nor for the pestilence that walketh in darkness; nor for the destruction that wasteth at noonday.

7A thousand shall fall at thy side, and ten thousand at thy right hand; but it shall not come nigh thee.

8Only with thine eyes shalt thou behold and see the reward of the wicked.

9Because thou hast made the Lord, which is my refuge, even the most High, thy habitation;

10There shall no evil befall thee, neither shall any plague come nigh thy dwelling.

11For he shall give his angels charge over thee, to keep thee in all thy ways.

12They shall bear thee up in their hands, lest thou dash thy foot against a stone.

13Thou shalt tread upon the lion and adder: the young lion and the dragon shalt thou trample under feet.

14Because he hath set his love upon me, therefore will I deliver him: I will set him on high, because he hath known my name.

15He shall call upon me, and I will answer him: I will be with him in trouble; I will deliver him, and honour him.

16With long life will I satisfy him, and shew him my salvation.

This Psalm portrays life's potential crises. A snare, terror, arrows, pestilence, destruction, people falling by the way, evil, a plague, a lion and an adder (poisonous snake) are the dangers lurking about. Perhaps we would never literally face a lion or arrows or such like, but the troubles we do face can be just as harmful and just as painful in their own ways.

The tremendous truth that stands out in this Psalm is that even though these pitfalls line our pathway, none of them can really destroy us as long as we walk with God. To be sure, they might set us back, but they cannot conquer us. Faithful followers of God have the Lord as their refuge and fortress. He is the cooling shadow in the noonday heat of Satan's angry attacks. He is like the mother hen who shelters her young from the storm. He is the deliverer and the protector.

As we read this Psalm and consider the application of its message, it's easy to think of the apostle Paul and the struggles he faced as a faithful Christian. He spoke of these difficulties twice in his second letter to the Lord's church in the city of Corinth.

In II Corinthians 4:8-9 Paul wrote, *"We are troubled on every side, yet not distressed; we are perplexed, but not in despair; Persecuted, but not forsaken, cast down, but not destroyed."* In Paul's mind, he could be touched by these challenges, but not defeated by them. Even though the troubles he faced left visible marks on his body (II Corinthians 4:10), his perspective on them is clearly seen a few verses later in his statement, *"For our light affliction, which is but for a moment, worketh for us a far more exceeding and eternal weight of glory."* (II Corinthians 4:17).

In II Corinthians 11:23-27 Paul penned these words by Divine inspiration:

> Are they ministers of Christ? (I speak as a fool) I am more; in labours more abundant, in stripes above measure, in prisons more frequent, in deaths oft. Of the Jews five times received I forty stripes save one. Thrice was I beaten with rods, once was I stoned, thrice I suffered shipwreck, a night and a day I have been in the deep; In journeyings often, in perils of waters, in perils of robbers, in perils by mine own countrymen, in perils by the heathen, in perils in the city, in perils in the wilderness, in perils in the sea, in perils among false brethren; In weariness and painfulness, in watchings often, in hunger and thirst, in fastings often, in cold and nakedness.

Paul considered none of these difficulties to be of permanent harm. Instead he saw them as opportunities to glorify God (II Corinthians 11:30).

Now let's return to the Psalm under discussion. Is the Psalmist saying that he would never have any trouble in life? After all, verse ten says, *"There shall no evil befall thee…"* We know that the Psalmist was not trouble free. If David was the writer, he had family troubles as well as difficulties brought about by foreign enemies and even his own countrymen. If this was written by a Psalmist during the Babylonian captivity, just being held as a prisoner in a foreign land was trouble enough.

Is the Psalm a guarantee of no problems in life? No. Is it a reminder that in the midst of all of these troubles stands our God as the watchman who will not allow us to be tempted beyond what we are able to bear? Yes. Is it a reassurance that God will keep a watch over us as we go through these challenges? Yes. Is it an affirmation that even though any one or even all of these dangers should befall us, we nonetheless cannot be permanently harmed by any trouble in this world because ultimately we will be delivered by the Lord, if not here, then in eternity? Indeed, it is.

As parents, we want our children to have all they need and to be safe. Because of our love for our children, we do all that we can to accomplish these ends in their lives. As our children grow, they begin to make their own decisions. Some are good while others are not so good. As we watch them mature, we give counsel and direction, but we do not so meticulously govern their lives that we rob them of their freedom. We do not keep them from everything that could harm them, but, as loving parents, we are always there for them when troubles come. This well illustrates the points made in the previous paragraph.

Notice verses 11 and 12. You might recall how Satan tried to misuse these in his face to face temptation of Jesus. "*Then the devil taketh him up into the holy city, and setteth him on a pinnacle of the temple, And saith unto him, If thou be the Son of God, cast thyself down: for it is written, He shall give his angels charge concerning thee: and in their hands they shall bear thee up, lest at any time thou dash thy foot against a stone.*" (Matthew 4:5-6). Satan's ploy was to persuade Jesus that God would not allow anything harmful to happen to Him. Even if He were to jump from the top of the temple, He would be rescued and would not suffer the slightest bruise, Satan suggested. Jesus knew that this was not the intent of Psalm 91. The Messiah understood that the Psalm was not a guarantee of a trouble-free life. Instead, the Lord showed His confidence in the fact that whatever harm Satan might try to cause, his efforts would have only temporary effects. "*Jesus said unto him, It is written again, Thou shalt not tempt the Lord thy God.*" (Matthew 4:7). Jesus knew the trouble He would face during His earthly tenure, but He also knew that He would have the victory in His faithful service to the Father.

What harm can life's troubles really do to us? They can discourage us. They can make us cry. They can cause stress. They can provoke fear and worry. If we allow them to turn us away from God they can lead us into much greater difficulties, even sin. But as we walk hand in hand with the Lord we again have to ask, "What can these trials and tribulations really do to us?" If we walk faithfully with the Lord and trust His will, can life's challenges really have any power over us?

Consider the power of these two rhetorical questions penned by inspiration in Psalm 27:1: "*The Lord is my light and my salvation; whom shall I fear? the Lord is the strength of my life; of whom shall I be afraid?*" Is there really anything in life that is so discouraging, so stressful, so heartrending that it can break us? "*There hath no temptation taken you but such as is common to man: but God is faithful, who will not suffer you to be tempted above that ye are able; but will with the temptation also make a way to escape, that ye may be able to bear it.*" (I Corinthians 10:13). Due to our human frailties, we may bend, but we need not break. Nothing can really harm us if we will trust God and faithfully follow Him.

Chapter Twelve
Psalm 93
The Comfort of Knowing That
God is Bigger Than Our Troubles

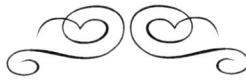

1The Lord reigneth, he is clothed with majesty; the Lord is clothed with strength, wherewith he hath girded himself: the world also is stablished, that it cannot be moved.
2Thy throne is established of old: thou art from everlasting.
3The floods have lifted up, O Lord, the floods have lifted up their voice; the floods lift up their waves.
4The Lord on high is mightier than the noise of many waters, yea, than the mighty waves of the sea.
5Thy testimonies are very sure: holiness becometh thine house, O Lord, for ever.

It's clear that this brief Psalm was written to extol the majesty of God. In it we also see at least by implication a marvelous contrast between the majestic God and the rulers of earthly kingdoms. Not only is God majestic, He is clothed (fully covered) in majesty as well as strength, as opposed to earthly rulers who are weak by comparison. Not only does He reign, He has always reigned (cf. Psalm 90:1-2), as opposed to the earthly rulers who would come and go. His words are always sure (sound and faithful) while the words of earthly rulers pass away. He is the very definition of holiness (I Peter 1:16), a trait greatly lacking in if not completely absent from the lives of the world's leaders.

Continuing his praise for the majesty of God, the Psalmist pays tribute to the Lord's awesome power. To say that God is stronger than literal floods is impressive. Indeed, He is that strong. Recall how Jesus calmed the boisterous sea in Matthew 14:22-33. It appears though that the Psalmist is striving to make a deeper impression. He wants to demonstrate that God is sovereign, that His majesty exceeds all earthly bounds. To that end, he uses the floods and noise of many waters to represent the troubles facing God's people. In the immediate context, reference is made to those nations who oppressed Israel. "Floods" is used in this manner in other passages (II Samuel 22:5; Psalm 18:4). "Noise" is also used in this fashion in Jeremiah 46:17 where the weeping prophet wrote that Pharaoh, king of Egypt, was only a noise, a temporary source of trouble. These figures are not limited to oppression from ungodly kingdoms though. In Psalm 69:2 David wrote in reference to his troubled life in general, "*I sink in deep mire, where there is no standing: I am come into deep waters, where the floods overflow me.*"

There appears to be a progression of danger in these figures. First come the floods, then the waves, then the noise of many waters, then the mighty waves of the sea. The floods are frightening enough, but when the lashing waves and their horrible din are added to the mix, the scene portrayed is one that can lead to fear and distress. Keep in mind though, that regardless of the power of these noisome waves, the Lord is mightier. Those who have ever seen video of or witnessed a tsunami can readily bring to mind a picture of an overpowering wave. Still, God is greater. He is clothed with majesty. He is bigger than any tempest, be it literally produced by the sea, or figuratively produced in our lives.

Because God is bigger than our troubles, He is quite capable of leading us through them. Not only that, He is fully acquainted with any difficulties we might face. Solomon wrote, "*The thing that hath been, it is that which shall be; and that which is done is that which shall be done: and there is no new thing under the sun.*" (Ecclesiastes 1:9).

God has witnessed every storm through which His people have passed. What's more, He has been by their side through every potentially perilous flood of trouble. He was with Joseph when the faithful patriarch was nearly murdered, sold by his brothers, mistreated by his master and forgotten by his friend (Genesis 37-50). He was with Hananiah, Mishael and Azariah when they were cast into the fiery furnace for their faith (Daniel 3). He stood by the side of Daniel in the lions' den (Daniel 6). Joseph was outnumbered and politically overpowered in his difficulties, yet the God who is bigger than our troubles delivered him. The three Hebrews faced the intimidating heat of a furnace that had been elevated to seven times its normal temperature, a temperature so high that the men who led the three to their intended doom perished in the flame (Daniel 3:19,22). In spite of this, the God who is bigger than our troubles delivered them. Daniel stood face to face with not one, but several lions. How many of those ferocious beasts were in that den is unknown to us, but certainly confronting even one of them would be frightening beyond words. Nonetheless, the God who is bigger than our troubles delivered Daniel.

We may never physically be in situations like those experienced by Joseph but emotionally we can feel outnumbered and overpowered by our troubles. We may never physically face the withering heat of a fiery furnace, but in our hearts we can feel the burn of distress and anguish. We may never physically stand among lions, but the fear and anxiety evoked by our troubles could be just as intense. Despite the enormity of the trials in which we may find ourselves, God is bigger.

There is nothing that burdens us that is too large to take to God. For that matter, there is nothing too small either. The familiar hymn says:

> O what peace we often forfeit,
> O what needless pain we bear,
> All because we do not carry
> Everything to God in prayer.

It's been said that if a thing is too small to take to God in prayer, then it is too small to worry about. If it is big enough to take to God in prayer and we have done that, then we should not worry about it.

When we approach God with our troubles, we are going to the one who is above us. "*For my thoughts are not your thoughts, neither are your ways my ways, saith the Lord. For as the heavens are higher than the earth, so are my ways higher than your ways, and my thoughts than your thoughts.*" (Isaiah 55:8-9). Our God is bigger than our troubles. What makes this truth even more comforting is the fact that this great God loves us (I John 4:9), cares for us (I Peter 5:7) and invites us to cast these burdens upon Him. *"Cast thy burden upon the Lord, and he shall sustain thee: he shall never suffer the righteous to be moved."* (Psalm 55:22).

Chapter Thirteen
Psalm 95
The Comfort of Fellowship In Worship

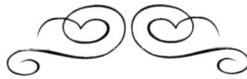

1O come, let us sing unto the Lord: let us make a joyful noise to the rock of our salvation.

2Let us come before his presence with thanksgiving, and make a joyful noise unto him with psalms.

3For the Lord is a great God, and a great King above all gods.

4In his hand are the deep places of earth: the strength of the hills is his also.

5The sea is his, and he made it: and his hands formed the dry land.

6O come, let us worship and bow down: let us kneel before the Lord our maker.

7For he is our God; and we are the people of his pasture, and the sheep of his hand. To day if ye will hear his voice,

8Harden not your heart, as in the provocation, and as in the day of temptation in the wilderness:

9When your fathers tempted me, proved me, and saw my work.

10Forty years long was I grieved with this generation, and said, It is a people that do err in their heart, and they have not known my ways.

11 Unto whom I sware in my wrath that they should not enter
into my rest.

Israel was invited to come together to worship God. The Lord had shown Himself worthy of praise and adoration. In what better way could the Israelites demonstrate their love and thankfulness to Him than in coming together as one in worship? Surely they would themselves be strengthened in the faith by banding together with a common focus and a common purpose with their worship being grounded in God's Word.

Their worship was directed to the one true God who was above all of the man made gods. They were to exalt the one who was their maker and their daily caretaker. Their hearts and minds were to be centered on the great God and King who held their eternity in His hands. What a powerful setting for honoring God and what a tremendous source of strength and comfort for the worshipers.

Worship has always been a vital part of the lives of God's people. We go back to the Patriarchal age and find faithful servants of God worshiping Him (Genesis 4:4; 12:8; 28:18-22, et al.). They worshiped Him during the Mosaic period (Exodus 20:1ff; et al.). Today faithful Christians worship him according to the New Testament pattern (John 4:23-24; Hebrews 10:24-25).

There are many blessings to be found in worshiping God. As it relates to the subject of comfort, one of these blessings is the fact that in worship we turn our attention away from self and toward the Lord. Comfort is hard to find if we only focus on ourselves and our sorrows. Turning to God in worship affords us the opportunity to look upward and set heart and mind on the one who can help us handle our troubles and provide the comfort we so desperately desire.

Fellowship is also rich in blessings. There are many "one another" passages in the Bible that show us how much we have to gain in fellowship with those of like precious faith (John 13:34; 15:12,17; Galatians 5:13; 6:2; Ephesians 4:2,32; Colossians 3:13,16; I Thessalonians 4:18; 5:11; Hebrews 3:13; 10:24,25; I Peter 1:22; I John 3:11,23; 4:7,11; II John 5). Paul seems to sum it up in his statement in Romans 12:10. "*Be kindly affectioned one to another with brotherly love; in honour preferring one another.*"

The combination of worshiping God and engaging in fellowship with His faithful children has two benefits. It allows us to direct our focus upward. At the same time we profit from the participation and encouragement of those around us who themselves are benefiting from their worship to the Lord. In short, gathering for worship is a marvelous tool for helping us handle life's troubles.

In this book I've tried not to give a lot of personal examples but I find it necessary here because of how much strength and comfort my wife, Shannon and I gained from this fellowship during her illness and how much I continue to benefit from it now that she's gone. Worshiping with the saints had long been a regular practice in our home as well as in the homes in which we grew up. Assembling with the church never became trite or boring. These times were opportunities to which we looked forward.

How well I remember one particular Sunday in the autumn of 2009. Due to her illness, Shannon had not been able to assemble with the church for worship for several weeks. On this particular Lord's Day she was well enough to go. As the first hymn began to be led, Shannon and I both joined in with the rest of the congregation. What her professionally trained voice lacked in strength at that moment was made up for with her heart. I looked at her as we sang. I'll never forget the smile on her face and the tears of joy in her eyes as she looked back at me. She was there in worship with the church. The soul-soothing strength it brought her could never be measured.

After Shannon's passing, I found myself, like all who grieve, having my good days and my bad days. I kept a daily journal of what I was feeling. After a couple of months I went back and read my entries and noticed a pattern. The best days I had in the time immediately following Shannon's death were Sundays and Wednesdays, those days of the week in which the church assembled for worship and Bible classes. The same is true as I write these words today.

The Lord knew there would be tremendous value in Christians worshiping together. That's why He commanded it. Paul wrote, *"Let us hold fast the profession of our faith without wavering; (for he is faithful that promised;) And let us consider one another to provoke unto love and to good works: Not forsaking the assembling of ourselves together, as the manner of some is; but exhorting one another: and so much the more, as ye see the day approaching."* (Hebrews 10:23-25). We know by example that the New Testament church met together for worship every first day of the week (Acts 20:7; I Corinthians 16:1,2). To be able on a regular basis to get away from the world and focus on our wonderful God and to do it with those who love Him and His Word is joyful and peaceful.

Chapter Fourteen
Psalm 102
Comfort In Prayer

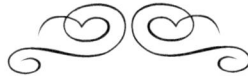

1Hear my prayer, O Lord, and let my cry come unto thee.
2Hide not thy face from me in the day when I am in trouble;
incline thine ear unto me: in the day when I call answer me
speedily.
3For my days are consumed like smoke, and my bones are
burned as an hearth.
4My heart is smitten, and withered like grass; so that I forget
to eat my bread.
5By reason of the voice of my groaning my bones cleave to my
skin.
6I am like a pelican of the wilderness: I am like an owl of the
desert.
7I watch, and am as a sparrow alone upon the house top.
8Mine enemies reproach me all the day; and they that are mad
against me are sworn against me.
9For I have eaten ashes like bread, and mingled my drink with
weeping.
10Because of thine indignation and thy wrath: for thou hast
lifted me up, and cast me down.
11My days are like a shadow that declineth; and I am withered
like grass.

12But thou, O Lord, shalt endure for ever; and thy remembrance unto all generations.

13Thou shalt arise, and have mercy upon Zion: for the time to favour her, yea, the set time, is come.

14For thy servants take pleasure in her stones, and favour the dust thereof.

15So the heathen shall fear the name of the Lord, and all the kings of the earth thy glory.

16When the Lord shall build up Zion, he shall appear in his glory.

17He will regard the prayer of the destitute, and not despise their prayer.

18This shall be written for the generation to come: and the people which shall be created shall praise the Lord.

19For he hath looked down from the height of his sanctuary; from heaven did the Lord behold the earth;

20To hear the groaning of the prisoner; to loose those that are appointed to death.

21To declare the name of the Lord in Zion, and his praise in Jerusalem.

22When the people are gathered together, and the kingdoms, to serve the Lord.

23He weakened my strength in the way; he shortened my days.

24I said, O my God, take me not away in the midst of my days: thy years are throughout all generations.

25Of old hast thou laid the foundation of the earth: and the heavens are the work of thy hands.

26They shall perish, but thou shalt endure: yea, all of them shall wax old like a garment; as a vesture shalt thou change them, and they shall be changed:

27But thou art the same, and thy years shall have no end.

28The children of thy servants shall continue, and their seed shall be established before thee.

This Psalm is titled, "A Prayer of the afflicted, when he is overwhelmed, and poureth out his complaint before the Lord." As was noted in another chapter, while the titles of the Psalms are uninspired, they nonetheless provide insight into at least some Bible readers' views of the gist of a Psalm. That this is a prayer is evident from the first verse. That this is a prayer pouring forth from an afflicted, overwhelmed heart is apparent from ensuing verses.

The misery being experienced by this Psalmist is seen in his assessment of his condition. Emotionally, he despairs of life (verse 3), his heart has taken a beating (verse 4) and he is lonely (verse 7). Physically, his anguish is so great that he can neither eat (verse 4) nor sleep (verse 7). His tears are many (verse 9).

If this is a captivity Psalm as some suggest, then the picture here is of one who is missing his homeland and is saddened by the actions that brought about his current state. He is discouraged by the apparent power of the enemies of God and perhaps even their arrogance. He looks forward in hope to restoration but in the meantime is pleading for God's comfort and care.

Throughout the Psalm there is a marvelous contrast between the brevity of the writer's life and the eternal nature of God. "*For my days are consumed like smoke…*" (verse 3). "*My days are like a shadow that declineth; and I am withered like grass. But thou, O Lord, shalt endure for ever; and thy remembrance unto all generations.*" (verses 11-12). Verses 24-27 draw out the contrast between the eternal God and His temporal creation. Verses 25 through 27 are quoted in the New Testament in Hebrews 1:10-12.

There is a beautiful formula to be found in Psalm 102. Take a person in distress, add that person's recognition of his own frailty, then add his realization of God's eternality, and finally add the hope that comes from a heart that trusts in God's care and the end result is fervent prayer.

Who can successfully deny the power of acceptable prayer as a source of comfort for the faithful child of God? Isn't prayer one of the first acts in which we engage when a trial comes upon us? Immediately we pray for relief from and removal of the difficulty. Often this initial prayer is little more than a silent utterance of "Lord, help me." When we meet life's challenges, we know we need to do something in response. Prayer is that response the vast majority of the time.

One of the reasons that prayer brings comfort is because it allows us to speak our minds. In the field of psychiatry this could be termed a catharsis, a "purging of the emotions or relieving of emotional tensions." Of course, perhaps the same could be said for shouting at a wall or standing on the beach and screaming at the ocean at the top of one's lungs. Either of those would provide a release, but neither effort has any definite direction. In prayer, we can "purge emotions" but faith that comes from the Word of God informs us that we are casting these emotions upon the Lord (I Peter 5:7). Long-term comfort comes from knowing that God is listening to the prayer of the broken-hearted Christian and, not only is He listening, He is answering. James wrote, "*The effectual fervent prayer of a righteous man availeth much.*" (James 5:16).

For what do Christians pray when in distress? Again, in sorrow's early stages we pray for things to change. We don't want to die or we don't want a loved one to die or we don't want to suffer. We want things to change. The apostle Paul wanted his thorn in the flesh to be removed (II Corinthians 12:8). Numerous prayers are found not only in the Psalms but in other works of inspired writers of the Old Testament where they were pleading for a release from their circumstances.

As we progress through the difficulty, we may still ask for things to change but we may also begin asking for the ability to accept the situation as it is and handle it more effectively. As Christians, we are concerned about our influence. We are also concerned about growing weaker in faith and allowing Satan to get an upper hand in our lives. Like Paul we could say, "*Lest Satan get an advantage of us: for we are not ignorant of his devices.*" (II Corinthians 2:11). We don't want him to use tragedy to deter us in our walk with God to heaven.

Also in prayer we might just want to pour out our hearts to the Lord. That seems to be what the author of this Psalm is doing. We don't see him asking God for anything other than an attentive ear and a speedy reply. He is just telling God what is on his mind. He's telling Him of his physical and emotional condition and speaking to Him of the daily persecution he faces from those who despise him.

Looking at this Psalm, we see one in trouble who devotes a portion of his prayer to praising God for his loving concern and precious promises. He expresses confidence in God's presence and protection.

To sum up this discussion of subjects for which a Christian might pray when in distress, we know that in prayer we can ask for a change in our situation, we can express a desire to be able to handle the circumstances so that they will not get the best of us spiritually, we can tell the Lord whatever is on our mind and we can offer Him praise from a heart filled with assurance of His power and love. Basically, we can talk to God about anything and everything. Since the prayers of faithful Christians are to God as "*golden vials full of odours*" (Revelation 5:8), we can "*come boldly unto the throne of grace, that we may obtain mercy, and find grace to help in time of need.*" (Hebrews

4:16). The question now is: Why would we NOT take "everything to God in prayer"? Why would we continue to carry burdens on our own shoulders rather than take them to God? With the power of prayer at the disposal of every faithful Christian, there is no good reason to keep any of our heartache bottled up inside.

There is a significant point to be made here regarding prayer. Just like the Psalmist's prayer was directed to the one true God and according to His will, our prayers must be offered in this same manner. John wrote, *"And this is the confidence that we have in him, that if we ask anything according to his will, he heareth us."* (I John 5:14). Our prayers must be directed to God the Father (John 16:23) through our Mediator, Jesus Christ (I Timothy 2:5).

When we pray as God instructed in His Word, are we guaranteed that we'll always get the result for which we ask? Of course we know that we will not. In this Psalm the writer recognizes the superiority of God. He writes with an understanding that God's will is greater than his. It's that faith that leads us to say as Jesus did in the Garden of Gethsemane, *"not my will, but thine, be done."* (Luke 22:42). That truly is one of the great points of comfort in prayer. We admit to the Lord that we don't know what to do, that we don't understand, that we are weak and infirm and we take comfort in the knowledge that we are speaking to the one who knows what to do, who understands and who is strong.

Sometimes we sing the words, "where could I go but to the Lord?" The theme of the song is that there is no other source than God for real strength, hope and comfort. An implied lesson that is just as powerful is the fact that while those outside of Christ have nowhere to turn in their search for comfort, Christians do have the Lord to whom we can go in prayer. Indeed, where else can we go when trouble strikes? Turning to God

Chapter Fifteen
Psalm 103
Comfort In Forgiveness

~❦~

1 Bless the Lord, O my soul: and all that is within me, bless his holy name.

2 Bless the Lord, O my soul, and forget not all his benefits:

3 Who forgiveth all thine iniquities; who healeth all thy diseases;

4 Who redeemeth thy life from destruction; who crowneth thee with lovingkindness and tender mercies;

5 Who satisfieth thy mouth with good things; so that thy youth is renewed like the eagle's.

6 The Lord executeth righteousness and judgment for all that are oppressed.

7 He made known his ways unto Moses, his acts unto the children of Israel.

8 The Lord is merciful and gracious, slow to anger, and plenteous in mercy.

9 He will not always chide: neither will he keep his anger for ever.

10 He hath not dealt with us after our sins; nor rewarded us according to our iniquities.

11 For as the heaven is high above the earth, so great is his mercy toward them that fear him.

12As far as the east is from the west, so far hath he removed our transgressions from us.

13Like as a father pitieth his children, so the Lord pitieth them that fear him.

14For he knoweth our frame; he remembereth that we are dust.

15As for man, his days are as grass: as a flower of the field, so he flourisheth.

16For the wind passeth over it, and it is gone; and the place thereof shall know it no more.

17But the mercy of the Lord is from everlasting to everlasting upon them that fear him, and his righteousness unto children's children;

18To such as keep his covenant, and to those that remember his commandments to do them.

19The Lord hath prepared his throne in the heavens; and his kingdom ruleth over all.

20Bless the Lord, ye his angels, that excel in strength, that do his commandments, hearkening unto the voice of his word.

21Bless ye the Lord, all ye his hosts; ye ministers of his, that do his pleasure.

22Bless the Lord, all his works in all places of his dominion: bless the Lord, O my soul.

Of all the words in the English language that lift the heart and lighten the soul, few can compare to "forgiveness." The word evokes thoughts of relief, freedom, and as it relates to eternal salvation, it brings to mind cancellation of the debt of sin provided to those who obey the Gospel of Jesus Christ.

The Psalmist's song demonstrates his appreciation of God's forgiveness. No matter how challenging life could become, no matter how many friends might forsake him, no matter how harsh his circumstances, he knew that God would redeem him, satisfy his soul and crown his life with loving kindness and tender mercies.

God's forgiveness is paramount, not only to our eternal welfare, but also to our success in overcoming life's troubles. As the writer says in verse ten, *"He hath not dealt with us after our sins; nor rewarded us according to our iniquities."* The apostle Paul wrote, *"There is none righteous, no not one"* (Romans 3:10) and *"For all have sinned, and come short of the glory of God."* (Romans 3:23). Were it not for God's forgiveness, our struggles with life's difficulties would be compounded by the burden of sin. There would be nowhere to turn. Paul said in defense of the resurrection of Christ from the dead, *"If in this life only we have hope in Christ, we are of all men most miserable."* (I Corinthians 15:19). If there is no forgiveness with God, we also have cause to walk through life in misery.

Consider the beautiful simile in verse twelve. If you were to start from where you are right now and travel north, you would go quite a distance and eventually reach the northernmost point of the globe. Upon taking your very next step, you would be heading southward. Were you to continue on this journey to the southernmost point of the globe, your very next step after you reached that point would be northward. On the other hand, were you to start from where you are right now and travel east, you would move in that direction indefinitely. Were you to begin traveling west, you would move in that direction indefinitely. East and west do not meet as north and south do. They are directions that are totally separate from one another. God's forgiveness causes the sins of one who obeys Him to be totally separated from the soul.

In verses fourteen through sixteen the writer reminds us of the brevity of life. Notice how he immediately follows that fact with the truth regarding the everlasting mercy of God toward them who fear and obey Him. Indeed, this God is eminently worthy of the multiple exhortations the Psalmist gives to "bless" (speak well of) the Lord.

While we're on the subject of forgiveness as it relates to comfort, let's briefly consider two other points. In both of these matters about to be discussed, if forgiveness does not take place, sorrow will swell and comfort will not come.

The first point is in regard to the need for each of us to forgive one another. Grudge-holding is a weighty burden that can rob a person of joy and peace. In Matthew 18:23-35 Jesus told a parable of two servants. One owed a great debt to his master. He begged for relief of the debt and his plea was granted. The other servant owed a small debt to the first servant. The first servant would not forgive that small debt. He had forgotten what his master had done for him. Jesus said, *"And his lord was wroth, and delivered him to the tormentors, till he should pay all that was due unto him. So likewise shall my heavenly Father do also*

73

unto you, if ye from your hearts forgive not every one his brother their trespasses." (Matthew 18:34-35). If we are the recipients of God's forgiveness, should we not be as generous with our forgiveness of others? *"And be ye kind one to another, tenderhearted, forgiving one another, even as God for Christ's sake hath forgiven you."* (Ephesians 4:32). True comfort can never come to the heart of one who is unwilling to forgive. How well I remember standing beside the hospital bed of an elderly lady who had spent years nursing a grudge against a family member. In the hours prior to her death, over and over again she quietly repeated, "God forgive me. God forgive me." She desperately sought the forgiveness that she herself had refused to grant for such a long time.

The second point concerns the need to forgive ourselves. One of the torments we suffer in the midst of life's difficulties is that of blaming ourselves for everything that has happened. Granted, sometimes our circumstances can be the result of our actions or lack of action. Even in those instances, if we seek God's forgiveness according to His will and He forgives us, we still need to learn how to forgive ourselves. What I'm talking about here though is the danger of constantly beating ourselves up regarding the difficulty in which we find ourselves. Anyone who has lost a loved one understands this. We all play "what if" in our minds until it nearly overwhelms us. It doesn't end the day of or even the week after the loved one's death either. Weeks, months, perhaps years later we might find ourselves questioning our decisions, wondering how things could have been different, tearing ourselves up emotionally over something over which, in reality, we had little or no control. We can't change the past. Why abuse our hearts with constant repetition of scenarios that never will happen?

Seeking forgiveness, extending forgiveness and accepting forgiveness form a magnificent triumvirate of comfort. When one knows that he or she is forgiven, there is nothing that can keep that person in despair.

Chapter Sixteen
Psalm 116
Comfort In Persistence

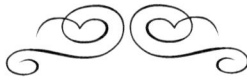

1love the Lord, because he hath heard my voice and my supplications.

2Because he hath inclined his ear unto me, therefore will I call upon him as long as I live.

3The sorrows of death compassed me, and the pains of hell gat hold upon me: I found trouble and sorrow.

4Then called I upon the name of the Lord; O Lord, I beseech thee, deliver my soul.

5Gracious is the Lord, and righteous; yea, our God is merciful.

6The Lord preserveth the simple: I was brought low, and he helped me.

7Return unto thy rest, O my soul; for the Lord hath dealt bountifully with thee.

8For thou hast delivered my soul from death, mine eyes from tears, and my feet from falling.

9I will walk before the Lord in the land of the living.

10I believed, therefore have I spoken: I was greatly afflicted:

11I said in my haste, All men are liars.

12What shall I render unto the Lord for all his benefits toward me?

13I will take the cup of salvation, and call upon the name
of the Lord.
14I will pay my vows unto the Lord now in the presence of
all his people.
15Precious in the sight of the Lord is the death of his saints.
16O Lord, truly I am thy servant; I am thy servant, and the
son of thine handmaid: thou hast loosed my bonds.
17I will offer to thee the sacrifice of thanksgiving, and will call
upon the name of the Lord.
18I will pay my vows unto the Lord now in the presence of
all his people,
19In the courts of the Lord's house, in the midst of thee, O
Jerusalem. Praise ye the Lord.

The first two verses of this Psalm speak of the writer's determination to follow God. The Lord heard him when he cried out for help. As the Psalmist phrased it, "*thou hast delivered my soul from death, mine eyes from tears, and my feet from falling.*" (verse 8). Having acknowledged this, the writer again expresses his determination to walk with God. "*I will walk before the Lord in the land of the living.*" (verse 9). In his sorrows, pains, trouble and afflictions, he found God. As was noted in another chapter, God was there for him at all times. He just needed to recognize the fact that he could go to the Lord at all times. When the Psalmist saw how great God had been to him in all of his difficulties, he stated his intention to be persistent in relying on the one who could deliver him in his struggles.

Again, this is noted in another chapter but it doesn't hurt to be reminded that God is there for us at all times just as He was for this inspired writer. The question is, "Are we looking for God at all times?" In our struggles, will we continue to try to handle them alone or will we turn to the God of all comfort?

In Luke's Gospel account we find two powerful parables illustrating the importance of persistence. In Luke 11:1-13 we find Jesus' disciples coming to Him with a request to teach them how to pray. He proceeded to give them the essentials of acceptable prayer in what is often titled, "The Lord's Prayer, but would be better called, "The Disciples' Prayer." Having said that, Jesus added an important component of prayer in verses five through eight when He gave an example of a person who continually asked a friend for something that he needed and eventually received it. The important component was and is persistence.

The other parable in Luke's account is in Luke 18:1-8. There Jesus tells of a woman who went over and over to a judge whom she trusted could handle a matter for her that she needed to have handled. In the parable, the judge granted her request. Verse eight asks a thought provoking question. *"Nevertheless when the Son of man cometh, shall he find faith on the earth?"* In other words, will the Lord see this type of persistence in the spiritual realm? Will those who claim to follow God through Christ be determined enough to go to Him at all times and in all situations? The comfort is there, as is the peace, the joy, the hope, the strength. Will we persist in our pursuit of God's blessings?

Life's challenges afford us abundant opportunity to show our faith in God, not only to others and to God Himself, but to ourselves as well. Have you ever wondered what you would do in a certain situation? Maybe you've been at the side of one who is struggling and either said or thought to yourself, "I don't know what I'd do if I were in your shoes." Not that we're looking for troubles, but when they do come (and they will), we are able to see for ourselves what we will do. We are also able to see for ourselves just how faithful the Lord can be to us if we will be faithful to Him. It's that persistence in the good times that aids us in being persistent in tough times.

It's interesting, but certainly not coincidental, that this Psalm contains the passage often heard at funerals. *"Precious in the sight of the Lord is the death of his saints."* (verse 15). In the context of a Psalm that shows the writer's commitment to God and God's commitment to him, this verse bespeaks the ultimate comfort that is found in turning to God. While on earth, the Psalmist realized God's comfort in a variety of situations. This life of daily faithfulness to God finds its reward in death. Rather than defeat, saints of God find victory in passing from this life to the next.

> So when this corruptible shall have put on incorruption, and this mortal shall have put on immortality, then shall be brought to pass the saying that is written, Death is swallowed up in victory. O death, where is thy sting? O grave, where is thy victory? The sting of death is sin; and the strength of sin is the law. But thanks be to God, which giveth us the victory through our Lord Jesus Christ. (I Corinthians 15:54-57).

Chapter Seventeen
Psalm 118
The Comfort of Knowing That I Will Win

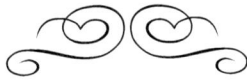

1O give thanks unto the Lord; for he is good: because his mercy endureth for ever.

2Let Israel now say, that his mercy endureth for ever.

3Let the house of Aaron now say, that his mercy endureth for ever.

4Let them now that fear the Lord say, that his mercy endureth for ever.

5I called upon the Lord in distress: the Lord answered me, and set me in a large place.

6The Lord is on my side; I will not fear: what can man do unto me?

7The Lord taketh my part with them that help me: therefore shall I see my desire upon them that hate me.

8It is better to trust in the Lord than to put confidence in man.

9It is better to trust in the Lord than to put confidence in princes.

10All nations compassed me about: but in the name of the Lord will I destroy them.

11They compassed me about; yea, they compassed me about: but in the name of the Lord I will destroy them.

12They compassed me about like bees; they are quenched as the fire of thorns: for in the name of the Lord I will destroy them.

13Thou hast thrust sore at me that I might fall: but the Lord helped me.

14The Lord is my strength and song, and is become my salvation.

15The voice of rejoicing and salvation is in the tabernacles of the righteous: the right hand of the Lord doeth valiantly.

16The right hand of the Lord is exalted: the right hand of the Lord doeth valiantly.

17I shall not die, but live, and declare the works of the Lord.

18The Lord hath chastened me sore: but he hath not given me over unto death.

19Open to me the gates of righteousness: I will go into them, and I will praise the Lord:

20This gate of the Lord, into which the righteous shall enter.

21I will praise thee: for thou hast heard me, and art become my salvation.

22The stone which the builders refused is become the head stone of the corner.

23This is the Lord's doing; it is marvellous in our eyes.

24This is the day which the Lord hath made; we will rejoice and be glad in it.

25Save now, I beseech thee, O Lord: O Lord, I beseech thee, send now prosperity.

26Blessed be he that cometh in the name of the Lord: we have blessed you out of the house of the Lord.

27God is the Lord, which hath shewed us light: bind the sacrifice with cords, even unto the horns of the altar.

28Thou art my God, and I will praise thee: thou art my God, I will exalt thee.

29O give thanks unto the Lord; for he is good: for his mercy endureth for ever.

Despite the lengthiness of this Psalm, it really doesn't require a lot of comment regarding the comfort it provides for the hurting heart. Very simply, it is a Psalm of victory. A brief phrase in verse five ("*I called upon the Lord in distress*") and a few sentences in verses 10 through 13 show that the Psalmist had been suffering. Other than that, there is nothing but excitement in the writer's heart and exultation in his inspired words. He has seen the victory that God provides and He wants others to know of the merciful God who delivers the righteous from their troubles.

That victory is not found in the words of men. The power of princes cannot provide deliverance. Salvation is in Jehovah God. "*The right hand of the Lord*" (a term representing strength) is alone sufficient to free the faithful from whatever distresses them. The joy of salvation in the Lord is emphasized three separate times, with a prophecy of the Christ who would come and be the culmination of God's plan for salvation found in verse 22. The Psalmist urges adoration of the Father. He is the one true God. He alone is worthy of praise. He is the source of victory over the challenges of life, no matter what they may be or how or from whom they may come.

Doubtless there have been times when each of us wished we could know in advance the outcome of a situation. If we could only see how things were going to turn out, we would feel much better and more capable of handling the challenge as we wrestle with it. The fact is that we do know the outcome. We may not know the particulars, but we do "*know that all things work together for good to them that love God, to them who are the called according to his purpose.*" (Romans 8:28). We know that our challenges will make us stronger if we let them (II Corinthians 12:7-11; Philippians 4:11-13). We know that the Lord will be at our side through the battle and we are confident that He will be there at the end of it (Hebrews 13:5). We can say with the inspired writer, "*The Lord is on my side; I will not fear.*"

This Psalm is a microcosm of life as a whole. Life's distresses come at us, sometimes with the ferocity of the bees to which the writer refers in verse 12. The Lord has given His Word and has His ears open to the prayers of the faithful (Revelation 5:8). He will deliver again and again, lifting up the fallen, binding the wounds of those who hurt, cheering the hearts of the fainting. Each challenge will be overcome by those who walk faithfully with God and ultimately, life's biggest challenge, that of sin and its destructiveness, will be overcome in eternity (Revelation 14:13).

The Psalm is also a microcosm of the Bible as a whole. Does not victory stand out as the focal point of God's Word? Genesis 1:31 speaks of God's perfect creation. Soon marred by sin (Genesis 3:6), this creation appeared to be forever severed from fellowship with the Lord (Isaiah 59:1-2). But hope for victory is announced early on in Genesis 3:15. Throughout the pages of the Bible this hope is fostered through the words of inspired men. The Word contains numerous accounts of individuals rising, then falling and then rising again to be close to God. Finally, just before the pen of Divine inspiration was laid down once and for all, the apostle John wrote of ultimate victory in eternity in Revelation 22. Follow God's Word from beginning to end and you will see the path of victory for those who follow God.

If God can provide eternal victory over sin, can He not provide victory over the challenges we face in life? Must we allow the troubles of this life to defeat us? Yes, the struggles are real. Yes, the pain is intense. At times it seems that we will never get over it. But the faithful will win. The difficulties of life are short-lived. After enumerating some of the trials he had undergone, Paul wrote,

> For which cause we faint not; but though our outward man perish, yet the inward man is renewed day by day. For our light affliction, which is but for a moment, worketh for us a far more exceeding and eternal weight of glory; While we look not at the things which are seen, but at the things which are not seen: for the things which are seen are temporal; but the things which are not seen are eternal. For we know that if our earthly house of this tabernacle were dissolved, we have a building of God, an house not made with hands, eternal in the heavens. (II Corinthians 4:16-5:1).

Even if trials continue throughout life, ultimately there is a release and eternal relief for the faithful Christian.

The faithful will win. Why? Going back to the Psalm under consideration in this chapter, we find the following reasons:

- "he (God) is good"
- "his (God's) mercy endureth for ever"
- "The Lord is my strength and song, and is become my salvation."
- "The right hand of the Lord is exalted: the right hand of the Lord doeth valiantly."

"*The Lord is on my side; I will not fear.*" There is no distress so great, no sorrow so deep, no anguish so severe that Satan will not try to use it to turn us away from following God. He tried to turn Job's difficulties into a victory for evil. Many times he sought victory over Joseph (Genesis 37ff). He even tried his hand at defeating Jesus.

Much to Satan's chagrin, there is no distress so great, no sorrow so deep, no anguish so severe that God cannot provide the victory over it in the heart of the faithful Christian. The faithful will win. The sadness may linger and the heart may feel the pangs of grief for many a day or year, but the faithful will overcome.

Jesus said, "*These things I have spoken unto you, that in me ye might have peace. In the world ye shall have tribulation: but be of good cheer; I have overcome the world.*" (John 16:33). John himself would later write about overcoming. "*I write unto you, young men, because ye have overcome the wicked one...*" (I John 2:13). "*... and the word of God abideth in you, and ye have overcome the wicked one.*" (I John 2:14). "*Ye are of God, little children, and have overcome them: because greater is he that is in you, than he that is in the world.*" (I John 4:4).

As downtrodden and broken in heart as we might feel due to our troubles, faithful Christians will win. "*For whatsoever is born of God overcometh the world: and this is the victory that overcometh the world, even our faith.*" (I John 5:4). "*O give thanks unto the Lord; for he is good: for his mercy endureth for ever.*"

Chapter Eighteen
Psalm 120
Comfort Even In the Presence of Evil Influences

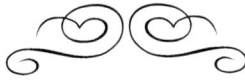

1In my distress I cried unto the Lord, and he heard me.
2Deliver my soul, O Lord, from lying lips, and from a
deceitful tongue.
3What shall be given unto thee? or what shall be done unto
thee, thou false tongue?
4Sharp arrows of the mighty, with coals of juniper.
5Woe is me, that I sojourn in Mesech, that I dwell in the tents of
Kedar!
6My soul hath long dwelt with him that hateth peace.
7I am for peace: but when I speak, they are for war.

In this Psalm the writer gives us a glimpse into the society in which he lived. He was surrounded by liars and deceivers whose false tongues inflicted pain and suffering upon the hearts of those subjected to their evil ways. It was a sorrowful situation in which he found himself. He wanted to live a peaceful,

God-fearing life but he was constantly at odds with those around him who desired an entirely different lifestyle. In spite of his many detractors, the Psalmist still found God and relied on Him for deliverance from his woes.

As strange as it may seem, there are those who will use another person's suffering as an opportunity to inflict even more pain. The phrase, "kicking a person while he's down" was not created out of thin air. Undoubtedly, someone who had felt the "kick" came up with that phrase.

The most obvious example of this "kicking" is found in the book of Job. Having lost his possessions, his children and even his health, Job was greeted by three men who are termed his friends in Job 2:11. At first it seems that they were sympathetic toward him in his loss. Job 2:12 reads, "*And when they lifted up their eyes afar off, and knew him not, they lifted up their voice, and wept; and they rent every one his mantle, and sprinkled dust upon their heads toward heaven.*" Job 2:13 says that they sat in silence with Job for seven days and nights "*for they saw that his grief was very great.*"

When Job finally opened his mouth, he spoke of his great sadness, even wishing that he had never been born (Job 3). Rather than allow his friend to vent his anguish and frustration over his losses, Eliphaz, one of the three, basically told Job, "I just have to say something." (Job 4:2). He spoke of how Job had helped others in their trouble and added, "*But now it is come upon thee, and thou faintest; it toucheth thee, and thou art troubled.*" (Job 4:5). Then Eliphaz delivered the key blow that emanated from the thoughts he had kept to himself for at least those seven days of silence. "*Remember, I pray thee, who ever perished, being innocent? or where were the righteous cut off? Even as I have seen, they that plow iniquity, and sow wickedness. reap the same.*" (Job 4:7-8). In other words, "Job, you are obviously getting what you deserve. No one suffers except they have done something terribly wrong." As the chapters of the book of Job go on we find Eliphaz, along with the other two friends, Bildad and Zophar, continuing their line of reasoning while Job defends his faithfulness to God.

Even though Job showed some weakness and was reprimanded by God for his attitude (Job 38-42), he nonetheless kept going back to the Lord in search of answers. He refused to renounce his faith, even though his wife encouraged him to do so (Job 2:9-10). Indeed, the Lord had well said of Job, "*there is none like him in the earth, a perfect and an upright man, one that feareth God, and escheweth evil.*" (Job 1:8).

Difficulties in life can come in a wide variety of forms. Physical illness or death of a loved one, our own physical illness, financial straits, discord in the home and issues on the job are just a few of the areas in which we can experience troubles. In each of these we do well in seeking comfort from the Lord. In each of these there is potential for those who would discourage us from so doing.

Here's a person who has lost a loved one to sudden death. As this one struggles to come to grips with the loss, he or she is confronted by friends and family who are angry and who are not taking their grief to God. They may say, "I can't believe you are taking this so calmly. How could you trust a God who would allow this to happen?"

Here's a person who has lost just about everything due to no fault of his or her own. As he or she commits this sorrow and anguish to God, friends and family begin to blame the person for poor business decisions. Others crank up the gossip machine and run it at full speed.

Here's someone whose family is in shambles. While that individual seeks God amidst the heartache of a broken home, friends and family point fingers. "This never would have happened if you would have ......" "I know what I would have done if my family had gotten like that."

Thankfully, there are countless numbers of friends and family who will stand with us and share in our requests to God for comfort. Nonetheless, we could encounter, as Job did, those who are *physicians of no value.*" (Job 13:4). Not only will they try to discourage us, they will try to change our focus and turn our eyes away from God.

The inspired writer of this Psalm found God even though those around him could not have cared less about the Lord. He cried out to the Lord in his distress and was heard.

Job found God even though his wife urged him to *"curse God, and die"* (Job 2:9) and his companions essentially told him that God wanted nothing to do with so vile a sinner. Job 42:12 opens with, *"So the Lord blessed the latter end of Job more than the beginning."*

When we face life's troubles, we can find the God of all comfort just as easily as we can find Him in good times, no matter what those around us may say or do. As Jesus said, *"Ask, and it shall be given you; seek, and ye shall find; knock, and it shall be opened unto you. For every one that asketh receiveth; and he that seeketh findeth; and to him that knocketh it shall be opened."* (Matthew 7:8-9).

"Let all those that seek thee rejoice and be glad in thee: let such as love thy salvation say continually, The Lord be magnified." (Psalm 40:16).

Chapter Nineteen
Psalm 121
Comfort In God's Preservation

1I will lift up mine eyes unto the hills, from whence
cometh my help.
2My help cometh from the Lord, which made heaven and earth.
3He will not suffer thy foot to be moved: he that keepeth
thee will not slumber.
4Behold, he that keepeth Israel shall neither slumber nor sleep.
5The Lord is thy keeper: the Lord is thy shade upon thy
right hand.
6The sun shall not smite thee by day, nor the moon by night.
7The Lord shall preserve thee from all evil: he shall
preserve thy soul.
8The Lord shall preserve thy going out and thy coming in
from this time forth, and even for evermore.

What's most impressive about this Psalm is the number of times a single Hebrew word is used in just a few short verses. Six different times this particular word is used, twice being translated "keepeth," once "keeper" and three times "preserve." In the opening verses the writer acknowledges the source of any help he has received. The Lord above is the source. The God who made heaven and earth is the origin of true and sufficient help. This God shows His dedication to His followers by never turning away from them. He never rests but is ever watchful over His people. He is the keeper, the source of preservation for those who abide in Him.

The Hebrew word noted in the previous paragraph is found over 460 times in the Old Testament. It carries with it a broad array of definitions, but they all come down to the idea of guarding, observing, giving heed, watching, preserving and protecting. In essence, God is watching over His faithful followers.

In the chapter on Psalm 23 we considered the fact that God knows us. Perhaps there are some similarities between these two chapters in this book, but the emphasis here is more on the fact that God sees all in our lives. Psalm 23 implies that He sees all because it shows how the Lord provides all that we need. This Psalm devotes more of itself to plainly stating that God sees all.

Does God know when we hurt? Is He watching when bad things happen to His people? Is He aware of the struggles that we face in trying to adjust to the dramatic changes in our lives brought on by calamity? The repetition of the word that shows God is watching, observing and giving heed to our lives indicates that He is indeed aware of every moment in our lives, be it good or bad. Such a thought was warmly welcomed by this Psalmist. He knew where to find God. He knew that God saw him in the day time and in the evening and whether he was going or coming. He took comfort in the knowledge that the ever-seeing eye of the Lord was aware of his every step. He took comfort in this because he knew that along with this watchfulness came the strength to stand firm and the preservation against evil. Nothing could really harm him as long as his God was watching over him. When he needed help, he knew where to find its source.

Knowing that God is ever present is disturbing to those who don't want Him to see what they're doing. To those who want to serve Him faithfully, such knowledge is worth more than any treasure on earth. While it is true that there is no sinful thought or evil deed that God does not see, so is it also true that there is no act of righteousness of which He is not aware and there is no twinge of sadness that is not laid bare before him.

Psalm 139 adds to the beauty of this thought about God's omnipresence and omniscience. There the Psalmist wrote:

> Whither shall I go from thy spirit? or whither shall I flee from thy presence? If I ascend up into heaven, thou art there: if I make my bed in hell, behold, thou art there. If I take the wings of the morning, and dwell in the uttermost parts of the sea; Even there shall thy hand lead me, and thy right hand shall hold me. If I say, Surely the darkness shall cover me; even the night shall be light about me. (Psalm 139:7-11).

God sees when we hurt. Some might wonder that since this is the case, why doesn't God do something to prevent the hurt. After all, is the Psalmist not saying here that God will keep His people from all things harmful? That's a good question. Is he suggesting that God suspends all laws of nature in order to keep anything bad from happening to His people? Is he indicating that God puts a halt to the aging process so that no one will ever get sick, grow old and die?

What the Psalmist seems to be saying is that while God watches over us physically, He preserves, guards and protects us spiritually. The former is obvious because the Psalmist is writing to living people. The latter is determined by the context, especially verse seven in which he has written, "*he shall preserve thy soul.*" God is watching over us and He will preserve, guard, and give heed to the spiritual welfare of those who rely on Him. Philippians 4:6-7 attests to this. "*Be careful for nothing; but in every thing by prayer and supplication with thanksgiving let your requests be made known unto God. And the peace of God which passeth all understanding, shall keep your hearts and minds through Christ Jesus.*"

As much as the difficulties of life hurt, they don't have to destroy us. The challenges will come and God sees when they do come, but He has established His guard to preserve us during these times. The troubles may become intense, but they will not smite our souls if we keep a firm foothold in God's Word. No matter where we may go, no matter how long we may live, we will have God's preservation of our souls if we faithfully obey His Word.

God's constant watchfulness and loving preservation are two facts that support the inherent power that lies in acceptable prayer. In Hebrews 4:13 Paul wrote, "*Neither is there any creature that is not manifest in his sight: but all things are naked and opened unto the eyes of him with whom we have to do.*" Since God is always watching us, then He is always near in prayer. Paul said, "*That they should seek the Lord, if haply they might feel after him, and find him, though he be not far from every one of us.*" (Acts 17:27). The Lord is not far off. Paul wrote in Philippians 4:5 that He is at hand. We may not be able to see Him, but He can see us.

After we've suffered a tragedy in our lives, who among us can tell when and where the pains of sadness will strike? We could go for days feeling happy and content and then suddenly, a song, a scent, a picture, practically anything could usher in a wave of sorrow and a rush of tears. As is clearly indicated in Psalm 121, God is there and He sees that. Since He is there, He is available in prayer. We can express the depths of our sorrow to Him in prayer and supplication, assured that He is dedicated to the preservation of our souls.

Chapter Twenty
Psalm 130
Comfort In Waiting For the Lord

1Out of the depths have I cried unto thee, O Lord.

2Lord, hear my voice: let thine ears be attentive to the voice of my supplications.

3If thou, Lord, shouldest mark iniquities, O Lord, who shall stand?

4But there is forgiveness with thee, that thou mayest be feared.

5I wait for the Lord, my soul doth wait, and in his word do I hope.

6My soul waiteth for the Lord more than they that watch for the morning: I say, more than they that watch for the morning.

7Let Israel hope in the Lord: for with the Lord there is plenteous redemption.

8And he shall redeem Israel from all his iniquities.

It may seem rather curious for a book devoted to comfort to contain a chapter about patience. What could one possibly have to do with the other? The answer is simple. Have you ever been impatient? If so, then you know the DIScomfort of stress. Impatience feeds anxiety while patience fosters trust which, in turn, brings comfort.

Nothing tests our patience more than life's challenges. We don't want to hurt. We want relief and we want it now. The trouble is that too often we expect life to be like a television show. A typical thirty or sixty minute program begins with a problem, proceeds to show that problem being addressed and then closes with it being solved, all within that time frame. Life should be so easy. The fact is though that relief from the difficulties we are facing frequently takes time to develop, thus demanding patience with God, with others and with ourselves.

This Psalm begins with the writer in those familiar depths which have been mentioned in other Psalms and which we ourselves have experienced. How many times have we felt that our hearts had reached the lowest regions of despair? The positive side of finding ourselves in such a state is that if we have hit the bottom, there's nowhere to go but up! This is the Psalmist's attitude. From his depths he doesn't look down to see how much further he might fall. Instead he looks above to the Lord whom he trusts to deliver him from his miry pit of sorrow. He pleads for the Lord's attention. He counts on the Lord in His mercy to open His ears and answer his prayer. With that in mind, he expresses the patience that is the theme of the Psalm and the focus of this chapter. Because he is calling upon the merciful God, the Psalmist is willing to be patient for an answer. He will be like one who through the night anxiously looks forward to the sunrise, but he will be patient because of his trust in the Lord.

Other chapters in this book have referenced the goodness of God in caring for His people. We only make note of it here so as to show it as the foundation of the patience that leads to comfort. Without the loving and merciful God there would be no reason for patience because we could not expect anything good to happen to us. A cruel, vicious God would offer no hope or promise of relief from life's difficulties and would leave us nothing good to anticipate. The God of creation, however, cares for His faithful ones. As a result, we know that He will give what is best and we patiently walk with Him in this confidence.

It's strange to hear people talking about "getting over" a difficulty that they've faced. Do we ever really "get over" a tragedy or does the intensity of it just lessen as time moves us away from it? In the newness of the tragedy we are consumed by its pain and its almost surreal nature. In the days that follow we have flashbacks of scenes of the tragedy and the people involved. We go through many moments of questioning why it happened and wondering if we could have done something to stop it. If the tragedy is the death of a loved one, we may even wonder why it wasn't us who died. Ensuing weeks run us through a wide range of emotions from anger to guilt to loneliness (especially in the loss of a loved one). It may be only days after the event in which we begin to wonder if we'll ever feel happy again or if we'll ever be able to get that tragedy out of our minds. Certainly as the weeks pass and we still find ourselves thinking about what happened, our desire to move on and not keep replaying the past in our minds grows stronger. Will we ever "get over" it? When the patriarch Jacob thought his beloved son, Joseph had been killed, he said, "*I will go down into the grave unto my son mourning.*" (Genesis 37:35). He did not see himself ever being able to overcome his grief.

The pain can lessen, especially as we turn to God for the comfort that He provides. All of the Psalms that are the subject of the study of this book, along with countless other inspired scriptures, serve to bring us to that "*peace of God, which passeth all understanding.*" (Philippians 4:7). But does the pain go away the moment we start reading God's Word? Do the tears of sorrow dry up immediately upon going to God in prayer? Because we still hurt days, weeks, months or even years after a death or some other tragedy in our lives, does this mean that we are weak in faith? Does it mean that God's Word is not as comforting as it is made out to be? Think about this: Every one of the Psalms being considered in this book is couched in the individual writer's need for comfort. Each writer is hurting in some way. Many of these Psalms were written by one man, King David. His pain sometimes lingered. God's deliverance was sometimes not immediate. Does that mean that David did not have faith or that God was not being good to him? No, what it means is that sometimes the relief that God provides takes time. In some of the Psalms, the writers wanted relief from the oppression of the enemy. In God's master plan, this would take time. In our lives, there may be greater good that can arise from our suffering (see Job). Comfort comes and will continue to come, but the lessening of the pain may take time.

Have you ever broken a bone? If you have and you are like most people, you were in pain. How long did it take for the pain to go away? Was it immediate? Even after the medicine and the extra attention you got, you still knew you had a broken bone as that cast was a constant reminder. Even as that cast was working to mend your bone, did you not from time to time feel the discomfort of that cumbersome annoyance? As much as you wanted the bone to mend immediately, you knew it would take time. The same is true of a broken heart. It can take time to mend. How long does it take? The answers to that question are as many in number as the people of whom it is asked. One of my Gospel preacher friends who had lost his wife to cancer told me when my wife, Shannon died, "Don't let anyone tell you how to grieve." That was sage advice. While we in our sorrow are trying to practice patience in our recovery, we must not allow others to rush us through the process. We need time. We need to work through the challenges we face.

In waiting for the Lord, we are not sitting around expecting Him to miraculously stir us out of our sadness. Throughout the Psalm, action is combined with the waiting. While waiting, the Psalmist is praying and consulting God's Word, the source of his hope (verse 5). James gives an interesting instruction regarding patience. *"But let patience have her perfect work, that ye may be perfect and entire, wanting nothing."* (James 1:4). Let patience work. Let it develop. Why? The reason is because the more we patiently seek God, the stronger we become spiritually and emotionally. This is a wonderful combination. Sitting around and doing nothing, looking inward at our sorrow rather than upward for our relief, will certainly lead to depression. On the other hand, the more we turn to God the more patience we develop and the more faith we build. Job said, *"But he knoweth the way that I take: when he hath tried me, I shall come forth as gold."* (Job 23:10). Peter wrote, *"That the trial of your faith, being much more precious than of gold that perisheth, though it be tried with fire, might be found unto praise and honour and glory at the appearing of Jesus Christ."* (I Peter 1:7). Let patience work. Allow your faith and trust in God to grow through the patience that you are developing and allow your patience to develop through your faith and trust in God.

While waiting for the Lord means that we trust Him to care for us in our sorrow, it also means that we don't try to get ahead of Him. Some in their sadness turn away from God, blaming Him for what happened. Some become despondent and just give up. Some turn to drugs. Some even take their own lives. God's *"divine power hath given unto us all things that pertain unto life and godliness, through the knowledge of him that hath called us to glory and virtue."* (II Peter 1:3). We have all that we need from Him. The Word that God has given us will work to comfort us if we will continually go to it and patiently apply it.

There are two other verses in the Psalms that echo the sentiment of Psalm 130. The first is Psalm 27:14. *"Wait on the Lord: be of good courage, and he shall strengthen thine heart: wait, I say, on the Lord."* Have you as a parent ever told your child to do something and then repeated it for emphasis? "Son, do your homework. I said, do your homework." It's obvious that in this instruction to your child you were expressing how important it was for him to do what you said. That's the motivation behind Psalm 27:14. *"Be patient. Don't get ahead of God. Be strong in Him. He will be there for you. Be patient, I said."* That's a great verse. Now read it again and compare it to the Psalmist's words in Psalm 130, especially verses five and six. In Psalm 27 we find an exhortation to wait. In Psalm 130:5-6, we find the commitment to wait. Not just once or twice but three times this Psalmist says he will wait. As he waits, he hopes, knowing full well the goodness of God.

The other verse that expresses the thought of Psalm 130 is Psalm 46:10. *"Be still, and know that I am God: I will be exalted among the heathen, I will be exalted in the earth."* The scene that immediately comes to my mind when I read this verse is that of Moses and the Israelites as they stood on the banks of the Red Sea with the Egyptian army in hot pursuit. Afraid that they were trapped and were about to be destroyed by the Egyptians, the masses cried out. In reply, *"Moses said unto the people, Fear ye not, stand still, and see the salvation of the Lord, which he will shew to you today: for the Egyptians whom ye have seen to day, ye shall see them again no more for ever. The Lord shall fight for you, and ye shall hold your peace."* (Exodus 14:13-14). The idea of being still in both settings seems to be that of ceasing to be stressed. Be still. Calm down. Be patient. Trust God. As this applies to those in sorrow, the message is regarding the need to not fret. Even though your world seems to be crumbling, God is still there. His Word is still powerful. He will still hear the prayers of the faithful. In His providence He is still active in this world. Be patient. You will find the comfort you crave.

The effort that we put forth to develop patience in the face of life's challenges is well worth the results. As is true in so many other Psalms, this one speaks of a reward for patience that is far above what any trust in earthly things could produce. To the original readers, the promise was that of not just redemption, but plenteous redemption. The abundance of God's blessings cannot be measured. In our patience we will find plenteous comfort.

Chapter Twenty-One
Psalm 139
Comfort "24/7/365"

1O Lord, thou hast searched me, and known me.
2Thou knowest my downsitting and my uprising, thou understandest my thought afar off.
3Thou compassest my path and my lying down, and art acquainted with all my ways.
4For there is not a word in my tongue, but, lo, O Lord, thou knowest it altogether.
5Thou hast beset me behind and before, and laid thine hand upon me.
6Such knowledge is too wonderful for me; it is high, I cannot attain unto it.
7Whither shall I go from thy spirit? or whither shall I flee from thy presence?
8If I ascend up into heaven, thou art there: if I make my bed in hell, behold, thou art there.
9If I take the wings of the morning, and dwell in the uttermost parts of the sea;
10Even there shall thy hand lead me, and thy right hand shall hold me.
11If I say, Surely the darkness shall cover me; even the night shall be light about me.

12Yea, the darkness hideth not from thee; but the night shineth
as the day: the darkness and the light are both alike to thee.
13For thou hast possessed my reins: thou hast covered me
in my mother's womb.
14I will praise thee; for I am fearfully and wonderfully made:
marvelous are they works; and that my soul knoweth right well.
15My substance was not hid from thee, when I was made in
secret, and curiously wrought in the lowest parts of the earth.
16Thine eyes did see my substance, yet being unperfect; and in
thy book all my members were written, which in continuance
were fashioned, when as yet there was none of them.
17How precious also are thy thoughts unto me, O God! how
great is the sum of them!
18If I should count them, they are more in number than the
sand: when I awake, I am still with thee.
19Surely thou wilt slay the wicked, O God: depart from me
therefore, ye bloody men.
20For they speak against thee wickedly, and thine enemies
take thy name in vain.
21Do not I hate them, O Lord, that hate thee? and am not I
grieved with those that rise up against thee?
22I hate them with perfect hatred: I count them mine enemies.
23Search me, O God, and know my heart: try me, and
know my thoughts:
24And see if there be any wicked way in me, and lead me in
the way everlasting.

Israel was surrounded by idolatry. Whether it was the nations around them
when they were free, the Babylonian society when they were in captivity, or
some of their own people in both settings, they were well acquainted with the
gods that man had created. Each of these gods was limited in its capacity. For
a good example of this, read the conflict between Elijah and the prophets of
Baal in I Kings 18. The mighty prophet of God challenged the false prophets

to call on their god to bring down fire from heaven. "*And they cried aloud, and cut themselves after their manner with knives and lancets, till the blood gushed out upon them. And it came to pass, when midday was past, and they prophesied until the time of the offering of the evening sacrifice, that there was neither voice, nor any to answer, nor any that regarded.*" (I Kings 18:28-29). The remainder of the chapter shows how Jehovah God responded to the request for fire from above.

In contrast to the false gods, the writer of Psalm 139 would have his readers understand that the true God is not limited in any way. There is not a time of day in which He is not present. There is not a thought or word that can be hidden from Him. Darkness cannot cloak the actions of His creation. The highest heights and deepest depths find Him there.

Think about this great truth as it relates to comfort. There is no situation in our lives of which our God is unaware. There is no time or place in which we cannot seek God and find Him if we seek Him according to His will (I John 5:14-15). His Word is at our fingertips. His merciful ear is open to the prayers of the faithful (Psalm 34:15). He will not sleep (Psalm 121:3). He will not go on a journey to a distant land in which He cannot hear (Acts 17:27-28). Lovingly and tenderly He says to His faithful ones, "*I will never leave thee, nor forsake thee.*" (Hebrews 13:5).

When we're struggling with life's troubles, it's amazing how quickly we can go from a high to a low. One day we can be on top of the world with everything appearing to be going our way. The next day we can feel as though we've been abandoned. There are so many factors that contribute to these seemingly sudden changes. A physical illness could dull our senses. Something we hear, something we see or even something we smell could bring to mind a sad thought. Anyone who has lost a loved one knows how this feels. A certain song comes on the radio and immediately you're transported back to the time when you and that loved were listening to that song together. You want the memory to make you happy and perhaps it does for a moment, but then you begin missing your beloved. A certain smell wafts through the air and it's almost as if the one with whom you associate that smell is in the room with you. Sadness ensues when you realize that he or she is not there. There are so many things that can trigger sadness but no matter where or when they happen, we have the God of all comfort at our side.

When this Psalmist considered the omnipresence of God, he wrote, "*Such knowledge is too wonderful for me.*" (verse 6). The word "wonderful" means "incomprehensible, extraordinary." When he talks about dwelling "*in the uttermost parts of the sea,*" in verse nine, he immediately follows that consideration with, "*Even there shall thy hand lead me, and thy right hand shall hold me.*" In verse eighteen, after commenting on God's thoughts, the writer says, "*when I awake, I am still with thee.*" God was there when the Psalmist went to sleep, while he slept and when he arose in the morning. He was there, as we say in our terminology, "24/7/365."

How marvelous it is to consider the fact that we can find God any time of day or night. When troubles strike or when the residual pain of these troubles rears its ugly head, we can turn to God and find Him there. Let us not deprive ourselves of this great blessing by limiting our contact with God to a building or an assembling with the church for worship. Saying this does not diminish the importance of worshiping with the saints (see this book's chapter on Psalm 95). It's just that we should not think of God as being confined to a certain place. When Solomon dedicated the temple to God he said, "*But will God indeed dwell on the earth? behold, the heaven and heaven of heavens cannot contain thee; how much less this house that I have builded?*" (I Kings 8:27).

Israelite parents were taught how to bring their children up in God's way. They were told, "*And these words, which I command thee this day, shall be in thine heart: And thou shalt teach them diligently unto thy children, and shalt talk of them when thou sittest in thine house, and when thou walkest by the way, and when thou liest down, and when thou risest up.*" (Deuteronomy 6:6-7). They were to instruct their children in righteousness at home, in their travels, at night and in the morning. When we need the comfort that only God can supply, may we follow this example and also seek Him when we're at home, when we're away from home, at night time and in the day. In other words, let us never limit our contact with the infinite source of comfort for He is there for us "24/7/365."

Chapter Twenty-Two
Psalm 142
Comfort In My Refuge

1I cried unto the Lord with my voice; with my voice unto the Lord did I make my supplication.

2I poured out my complaint before him; I shewed before him my trouble.

3When my spirit was overwhelmed within me, then thou knewest my path. In the way wherein I walked have they privily laid a snare for me.

4I looked on my right hand, and beheld, but there was no man that would know me: refuge failed me; no man cared for my soul.

5I cried unto thee, O Lord: I said, Thou art my refuge and my portion in the land of the living.

6Attend unto my cry: for I am brought very low: deliver me from my persecutors; for they are stronger than I.

7Bring my soul out of prison, that I may praise thy name: the righteous shall compass me about; for thou shalt deal bountifully with me.

Although the titles that appear prior to many of the Psalms are not inspired, they do provide insight into the view of some regarding the various settings. The title of Psalm 142 suggests that it was penned by David when he was in a cave. The cross reference is to I Samuel 22:1. *"David therefore departed thence, and escaped to the cave Adullam: and when his brethren and all his father's house heard it, they went down thither to him."* This cave was one of the places in which David found himself after he fled from murder-minded King Saul. Psalm 57 carries a similar title.

The Psalm doesn't require the title in order for it to be a meaningful source of comfort. If the title is appropriate, then it shows a man who, though having sought refuge in a cave, actually found there little more than a hiding place from one who was seeking his life. It did not provide him a hiding place from the sorrow that burdened his soul. Regardless of the exact setting of the Psalm, it emanated from a troubled heart.

The key aspect of this Psalm as a source of comfort is in the contrast presented in verses three and four. The writer looked to his fellow man for help but found none. He just wanted someone on whom he could rely. One who would be on another's right hand would typically be his most trustworthy friend, his most dependable confidant. This confidant would provide the place of refuge or escape from the enemy. If this was indeed David writing this as he was on the run from Saul, then we can understand his anguish as just prior to entering the cave he had parted company with his best friend, Jonathan and would never see him alive again (I Samuel 20:41-42). There was no longer anyone on earth to whom he could go to escape from the troubles he was facing.

On the other hand, God was there to give him the shelter from danger that he so intensely desired. There was no real help in man. If he wanted to escape his troubles and find refuge, he would find it only in God.

When we face difficulties, we too need a refuge. Sometimes we just need to get away. We need a break from all of the burdens that are mounting up. We need an escape. God is that escape. He is the source of strength, of constant spiritual energy. We need time with Him. We need time alone with Him.

Jesus knew the value of this time alone with God. Matthew 14:23 says, *"And when he had sent the multitudes away, he went up into a mountain apart to pray: and when the evening was come, he was there alone."* Luke tells us, *"And it came to pass in those days, that he went out into a mountain to pray, and continued all night in prayer to God."* (Luke 6:12). With the agony of the cross and all that surrounded it looming before Him, Jesus went alone into the Garden of Gethsemane and poured out His heart to the Father (John 17).

The irony of this need to escape to our refuge and spend time with Him alone in prayer and meditation of His Word is that well-meaning friends and family sometimes don't want to allow sufferers this time. More than likely they are just concerned about the one who is troubled. Maybe they're afraid that the sufferer will harm himself or herself if left alone. Maybe they're concerned that the burden will be too great for the person to handle alone. Those dangers could indeed exist in some cases, but many times, those moments alone with God are the most significant in the comfort and even the spiritual growth of the one who is troubled.

A sufferer can be surrounded by family and friends and suddenly feel the need to get away for some quiet time. This is not a reflection on those who are trying to help. In fact, as odd as it may seem, the sufferer may already be alone in his or her thoughts, even in a crowded room. Those who have experienced grief and sorrow know all about this. They know what it's like to feel isolated in a roomful of people, to hear voices but not words, to see shapes but not faces.

The one who is suffering should feel no shame in needing to get away. He or she should not feel the need to apologize for needing to get away, nor should anyone apologize for that person. The one who is suffering just needs refuge. Yes, even in the midst of the closest of friends and family, the sufferer may need to break away and spend time with the only one who truly understands the intensity of the pain and who alone can provide the depth of comfort required.

God is the refuge for the troubled soul. Other Psalms echo this fact. "*God is our refuge and strength, a very present help in trouble.*" (Psalm 46:1). "*In God is my salvation and my glory: the rock of my strength, and my refuge, is in God. Trust in him at all times; ye people, pour out your heart before him: God is a refuge for us. Selah.*" (Psalm 62:7,8). "*I will say of the Lord, He is my refuge and my fortress: my God; in him will I trust.*" (Psalm 91:2). "*But the Lord is my defense; and my God is the rock of my refuge.*" (Psalm 94:22).

Of course, one need not be alone to run to God for refuge. Prayer can be offered anytime and anywhere. Study of the Bible can take place anytime and anywhere. Times of worship with fellow Christians afford additional opportunities to go to God. Beyond this, however, the simple fact is that those who face challenges need time alone with God to be able to express their innermost feelings and deepest pain. Maybe there's even a special place to which one can go to have this time with God. A quiet room in the house, a special place that brings happy memories or any number of locations could provide the place to which one can go when he or she needs that time alone in communion with the Lord.

God is the place of shelter for the troubled soul. He is the one to whom we can run to escape the burdens of life's difficulties and gain the strength we need to go back out and face them. "*Cast thy burden upon the Lord, and he shall sustain thee: he shall never suffer the righteous to be moved.*" (Psalm 55:22).

Part Two
Individual Verses of Comfort

When facing difficulties, we need to regularly sit down and engage in extended meditation and contemplation of God's Word. There are times though that we may need just a quick reminder of the comfort that the Lord provides. The purpose of this part of the book is to aid the reader in finding these reminders. Any of the passages cited below would make excellent memory verses.

I Can Learn From My Troubles

- Psalm 119:67 – "Before I was afflicted I went astray: but now have I kept thy word."
- Psalm 119:71 – "It is good for me that I have been afflicted; that I might learn thy statutes."

I Can Have Confidence in God's Care

- Psalm 3:5 – "I laid me down and slept; I awaked; for the Lord sustained me."
- Psalm 4:8 – "I will both lay me down in peace, and sleep: for thou, Lord, only makest me dwell in safety."
- Psalm 27:3 – "Though an host should encamp against me, my heart shall not fear: though war should rise against me, in this will I be confident."

God Always Blesses Me In Abundance

- Psalm 13:6 – "I will sing unto the Lord, because he hath dealt bountifully with me."
- Psalm 16:11 – "Thou wilt shew me the path of life: in thy presence is fullness of joy; at thy right hand there are pleasures for evermore."
- Psalm 18:35 – "Thou hast also given me the shield of thy salvation: and thy right hand hath holden me up, and thy gentleness hath made me great."

- Psalm 25:6 – "Remember, O Lord, thy tender mercies and thy lovingkindnesses; for they have been ever of old."
- Psalm 25:10 – "All the paths of the Lord are mercy and truth unto such as keep his covenant and his testimonies."
- Psalm 34:8-10 – "O taste and see that the Lord is good: blessed is the man that trusteth in him. O fear the Lord, ye his saints: for there is no want to them that fear him. The young lions do lack, and suffer hunger: but they that seek the Lord shall not want any good thing."
- Psalm 36:7-9 – "How excellent is thy loving-kindness, O God! therefore the children of men put their trust under the shadow of thy wings. They shall be abundantly satisfied with the fatness of thy house; and thou shalt make them drink of the river of thy pleasures. For with thee is the fountain of life: in thy light shall we see light."
- Psalm 37:16-17 – "A little that a righteous man hath is better than the riches of many wicked. for the arms of the wicked shall be broken: but the Lord upholdeth the righteous."
- Psalm 40:5 – "Many, O Lord my God, are thy wonderful works which thou hast done, and thy thoughts which are to us-ward: they cannot be reckoned up in order unto thee: if I would declare and speak of them, they are more than can be numbered."
- Psalm 63:3 – "Because thy lovingkindness is better than life, my lips shall praise thee."
- Psalm 68:19 – "Blessed be the Lord, who daily loadeth us with benefits, even the God of our salvation. Selah."
- Psalm 84:11 – "For the Lord God is a sun and shield: the Lord will give grace and glory: no good thing will he withhold from them that walk uprightly."
- Psalm 86:15 – "But thou, O Lord, art a God full of compassion, and gracious, longsuffering, and plenteous in mercy and truth."
- Psalm 100:4-5 – "Enter into his gates with thanksgiving, and into his courts with praise: be thankful unto him, and bless his name. For the Lord is good; his mercy is everlasting; and his truth endureth to all generations."
- Psalm 103:8 – "The Lord is merciful and gracious, slow to anger, and plenteous in mercy."

- Psalm 107:8-9 – "Oh that men would praise the Lord for his goodness, and for his wonderful works to the children of men! For he satisfieth the longing soul, and filleth the hungry soul with goodness."
- Psalm 116:5 – "Gracious is the Lord, and righteous; yea, our God is merciful."
- Psalm 117:1-2 – "O praise the Lord, all ye nations: praise him all ye people. For his merciful kindness is great toward us: and the truth of the Lord endureth for ever. Praise ye the Lord."
- Psalm 118:29 – "O give thanks unto the Lord; for he is good: for his mercy endureth for ever."
- Psalm 126:3 – "The Lord hath done great things for us; whereof we are glad."
- Psalm 146:5 – "Happy is he that hath the God of Jacob for his help, whose hope is in the Lord his God."

God Can Deliver Me From My Troubles

- Psalm 17:7 – "Shew thy marvelous loving-kindness, O thou that savest by thy right hand them which put their trust in thee from those that rise up against them."
- Psalm 25:15 – "Mine eyes are ever toward the Lord; for he shall pluck my feet out of the net."
- Psalm 30:3 – "O Lord, thou hast brought up my soul from the grave: thou hast kept me alive, that I should not go down to the pit."
- Psalm 34:4-6 – "I sought the Lord, and he heard me, and delivered me from all my fears. They looked unto him and were lightened: and their faces were not ashamed. This poor man cried, and the Lord heard him, and saved him out of all his troubles."
- Psalm 34:17-19 – The righteous cry, and the Lord heareth, and delivereth them out of all their troubles. The Lord is nigh unto them that are of a broken heart; and saveth such as be of a contrite spirit. Many are the afflictions of the righteous: but the Lord delivereth him out of them all."
- Psalm 35:10 – "All my bones shall say, Lord, who is like unto thee, which deliverest the poor from him that is too strong for him, yea, the poor and the needy from him that spoileth him?"
- Psalm 40:1-2 – "I waited patiently for the Lord; and he inclined unto me, and heard my cry. He brought me up also out of an

horrible pit, out of the miry clay, and set my feet upon a rock, and established my goings."
- Psalm 66:12 – "Thou hast caused men to ride over our heads; we went through fire and through water: but thou broughtest us out into a wealthy place."
- Psalm 145:14 – "The Lord upholdeth all that fall, and raiseth up all those that be bowed down."
- Psalm 147:3 – "He healeth the broken in heart, and bindeth up their wounds."

There Is No One Like the God of the Bible

- Psalm 8:1 – "O Lord our Lord, how excellent is thy name in all the earth! who hast set thy glory above the heavens."
- Psalm 18:46 – "The Lord liveth; and blessed be my rock; and let the God of my salvation be exalted."
- Psalm 19:1-3 – "The heavens declare the glory of God; and the firmament sheweth his handywork. Day unto day uttereth speech, and night unto night sheweth knowledge. There is no speech nor language, where their voice is not heard."
- Psalm 29:3-4 – "The voice of the Lord is upon the waters: the God of glory thundereth: the Lord is upon many waters. The voice of the Lord is powerful; the voice of the Lord is full of majesty."
- Psalm 29:10 – "The Lord sitteth upon the flood; yea, the Lord sitteth King for ever."
- Psalm 33:16-17 – "There is no king saved by the multitude of an host: a mighty man is not delivered by much strength. An horse is a vain thing for safety: neither shall he deliver any by his great strength."
- Psalm 48:10 – "According to thy name, O God, so is thy praise unto the ends of the earth: thy right hand is full of righteousness."
- Psalm 60:11 – "Give us help from trouble: for vain is the help of man."
- Psalm 71:19 – "Thy righteousness also, O God, is very high, who hast done great things: O God, who is like unto thee!"
- Psalm 73:25 – "Whom have I in heaven but thee? and there is none upon earth that I desire beside thee."
- Psalm 77:14 – "Thou art the God that doest wonders: thou hast declared thy strength among the people."

- Psalm 90:1-2 – "Lord, thou hast been our dwelling place in all generations. Before the mountains were brought forth, or ever thou hadst formed the earth and the world, even from everlasting to everlasting, thou art God."
- Psalm 95:3-5 – "For the Lord is a great God, and a great King above all gods. In his hand are the deep places of the earth: the strength of the hills is his also. The sea is his, and he made it: and his hands formed the dry land."
- Psalm 96:4-6 – "For the Lord is great, and greatly to be praised: he is to be feared above all gods. For all the gods of the nations are idols: but the Lord made the heavens. Honour and majesty are before him: strength and beauty are in his sanctuary."
- Psalm 97:9 – "For thou, Lord, art high above all the earth: thou art exalted above all gods."
- Psalm 108:12 – "Give us help from trouble: for vain is the help of man."
- Psalm 113:2-6 – "Blessed be the name of the Lord from this time forth and for evermore. From the rising of the sun unto the going down of the same the Lord's name is to be praised. The Lord is high above all nations, and his glory above the heavens. Who is like unto the Lord our God, who dwelleth on high, Who humbleth himself to behold the things that are in heaven, and in the earth!"
- Psalm 118:8-9 – "It is better to trust in the Lord than to put confidence in man. It is better to trust in the Lord than to put confidence in princes."
- Psalm 135:5 – "For I know that the Lord is great, and that our Lord is above all gods."
- Psalm 147:5 – "Great is our Lord, and of great power: his understanding is infinite."

God Knows What's Happening In My Life

- Psalm 11:4 – "The Lord is in his holy temple, the Lord's throne is in heaven: his eyes behold, his eyelids try, the children of men."
- Psalm 24:1 – "The earth is the Lord's, and the fullness thereof; the world, and they that dwell therein."
- Psalm 31:7-8 – "I will be glad and rejoice in thy mercy: for thou hast considered my trouble; thou hast known my soul in adversities;

and hast not shut me up into the hand of the enemy: thou hast set my feet in a large room."

- Psalm 40:17 – "But I am poor and needy; yet the Lord thinketh on me: thou art my help and my deliverer; make no tarrying, O my God."

God Will Never Fail Me

- Psalm 3:3 – "But thou, O Lord, art a shield for me; my glory, and the lifter up of mine head."
- Psalm 37:23-24 – "The steps of a good man are ordered by the Lord: and he delighteth in his way. Though he fall, he shall not be utterly cast down: for the Lord upholdeth him with his hand."
- Psalm 5:11-12 – "But let all those that put their trust in thee rejoice: let them ever shout for joy, because thou defendest them: let them also that love thy name be joyful in thee. For thou, Lord, wilt bless the righteous; with favour wilt thou compass him as with a shield."
- Psalm 7:10 – "My defence is of God, which saveth the upright in heart."
- Psalm 9:9-10 – "The Lord also will be a refuge for the oppressed, a refuge in times of trouble. And they that know thy name will put their trust in thee: for thou, Lord, hast not forsaken them that seek thee."
- Psalm 17:8 – "Keep me as the apple of the eye, hide me under the shadow of thy wings."
- Psalm 18:30 – "As for God, his way is perfect: the word of the Lord is tried: he is a buckler to all those that trust in him."
- Psalm 27:5 – "For in time of trouble he shall hide me in his pavilion: in the secret of his tabernacle shall he hide me; he shall set me up upon a rock."
- Psalm 32:7 – "Thou art my hiding place; thou shalt preserve me from trouble; thou shalt compass me about with songs of deliverance. Selah."
- Psalm 32:10 – "Many sorrows shall be to the wicked: but he that trusteth in the Lord, mercy shall compass him about."
- Psalm 33:20 – "Our soul waiteth for the Lord: he is our help and our shield."
- Psalm 48:14 – "For this God is our God for ever and ever: he will be our guide even unto death."

- Psalm 57:1 – "Be merciful unto me, O God, be merciful unto me: for my soul trusteth in thee: yea, in the shadow of thy wings will I make my refuge, until these calamities be overpast."
- Psalm 62:1-2 – "Truly my soul waiteth upon God: from him cometh my salvation. He only is my rock and my salvation; he is my defence; I shall not be greatly moved."
- Psalm 62:6-7 – "He only is my rock and my salvation: he is my defence; I shall not be moved. In God is my salvation and my glory: the rock of my strength, and my refuge, is in God."
- Psalm 63:7 – "Because thou hast been my help, therefore in the shadow of thy wings will I rejoice."
- Psalm 73:23-24 – "Nevertheless I am continually with thee: thou hast holden me by my right hand. Thou shalt guide me with thy counsel, and afterward receive me to glory."
- Psalm 94:17-18 – "Unless the Lord had been my help, my soul had almost dwelt in silence. When I said, My foot slippeth; thy mercy, O Lord, held me up."
- Psalm 94:22 – "But the Lord is my defence; and my God is the rock of my refuge."
- Psalm 115:11 – "Ye that fear the Lord, trust in the Lord: he is their help and their shield."
- Psalm 116:7 – "Return unto thy rest, O my soul; for the Lord hath dealt bountifully with thee."
- Psalm 118:6 – "The Lord is on my side; I will not fear: what can man do unto me?"
- Psalm 121:2 – "My help cometh from the Lord, which made heaven and earth."
- Psalm 121:5-8 – "The Lord is thy keeper: the Lord is thy shade upon thy right hand. The sun shall not smite thee by day, nor the moon by night. The Lord shall preserve thee from all evil: he shall preserve thy soul. The Lord shall preserve thy going out and thy coming in from this time forth, and even for evermore."
- Psalm 124:8 – "Our help is in the name of the Lord, who made heaven and earth."
- Psalm 140:7 – "O God the Lord, the strength of my salvation, thou hast covered my head in the day of battle."

God Hears the Prayers of the Righteous

- Psalm 3:4 – "I cried unto the Lord with my voice, and he heard me out of his holy hill. Selah."
- Psalm 4:3 – "But know that the Lord hath set apart him that is godly for himself: the Lord will hear when I call unto him."
- Psalm 6:9 – "The Lord hath heard my supplication; the Lord will receive my prayer."
- Psalm 22:24 – "For he hath not despised nor abhorred the affliction of the afflicted; neither hath he hid his face from him; but when he cried unto him, he heard."
- Psalm 34:15 – "The eyes of the Lord are upon the righteous, and his ears are open unto their cry."
- Psalm 91:15 – "He shall call upon me, and I will answer him: I will be with him in trouble; I will deliver him, and honour him."
- Psalm 55:22 – "Cast thy burden upon the Lord, and he shall sustain thee: he shall never suffer the righteous to be moved."
- Psalm 86:7 – "In the day of my trouble I will call upon thee: for thou wilt answer me."
- Psalm 102:17 – "He will regard the prayer of the destitute, and not despise their prayer."
- Psalm 118:5 – "I called upon the Lord in distress: the Lord answered me, and set me in a large place."
- Psalm 145:18 – "The Lord is nigh unto all them that call upon him, to all that call upon him in truth."

God Is My Strength

- Psalm 18:2 – "The Lord is my rock, and my fortress, and my deliverer; my God, my strength, in whom I will trust; my buckler, and the horn of my salvation, and my high tower."
- Psalm 18:31 – "For who is God save the Lord? or who is a rock save our God?"
- Psalm 20:7 – "Some trust in chariots, and some in horses: but we will remember the name of the Lord our God."
- Psalm 21:1 – "The king shall joy in thy strength, O Lord; and in thy salvation how greatly shall he rejoice!"
- Psalm 27:1 – "The Lord is my light and my salvation; whom shall I fear? the Lord is the strength of my life; of whom shall I be afraid?"

- Psalm 28:7 – "The Lord is my strength and my shield; my heart trusted in him, and I am helped: therefore my heart rejoiceth; and with my song will I praise him."
- Psalm 28:8 – "The Lord is their strength, and he is the saving strength of his anointed."
- Psalm 31:3 – "For thou art my rock and my fortress; therefore for thy name's sake lead me, and guide me."
- Psalm 37:39 – "But the salvation of the righteous is of the Lord: he is their strength in the time of trouble."
- Psalm 46:1-3 – "God is our refuge and strength, a very present help in trouble. Therefore will not we fear, though the earth be removed, and though the mountains be carried into the midst of the sea; Though the waters thereof roar and be troubled, though the mountains shake with the swelling thereof. Selah."
- Psalm 73:26 – "My flesh and my heart faileth: but God is the strength of my heart, and my portion for ever."
- Psalm 59:9 – "Because of his strength will I wait upon thee: for God is my defence."
- Psalm 59:16-17 – "But I will sing of thy power; yea, I will sing aloud of thy mercy in the morning: for thou hast been my defence and refuge in the day of my trouble. Unto thee, O my strength, will I sing: for God is my defence, and the God of my mercy."
- Psalm 61:2-3 – "From the end of the earth will I cry unto thee, when my heart is overwhelmed: lead me to the rock that is higher than I. For thou hast been a shelter for me, and a strong tower from the enemy."
- Psalm 71:16 – "I will go in the strength of the Lord God: I will make mention of thy righteousness, even of thine only."
- Psalm 89:8 – "O Lord God of hosts, who is a strong Lord like unto thee? or to thy faithfulness round about thee?"
- Psalm 89:13 – "Thou hast a mighty arm: strong is thy hand, and high is thy right hand."
- Psalm 118:14 – "The Lord is my strength and song, and is become my salvation."

I Can Rely On God's Word
- Psalm 12:6 – "The words of the Lord are pure words: as silver tried in a furnace of earth, purified seven times."

- Psalm 19:7-8 – "The law of the Lord is perfect, converting the soul: the testimony of the Lord is sure, making wise the simple. The statutes of the Lord are right, rejoicing the heart: the commandment of the Lord is pure, enlightening the eyes."
- Psalm 25:5 – "Lead me in thy truth, and teach me: for thou art the God of my salvation; on thee do I wait all the day."
- Psalm 33:4 – "For the word of the Lord is right; and all his works are done in truth."
- Psalm 119:28 – "My soul melteth for heaviness: strengthen thou me according unto thy word."
- Psalm 119:49-50 – "Remember the word unto thy servant, upon which thou hast caused me to hope. This is my comfort in my affliction: for thy word hath quickened me."
- Psalm 119:92-93 – "Unless thy law had been my delights, I should then have perished in mine affliction. I will never forget thy precepts: for with them thou hast quickened me."
- Psalm 119:105 – "Thy word is a lamp unto my feet, and a light unto my path."
- Psalm 119:114 – "Thou art my hiding place and my shield: I hope in thy word."
- Psalm 119:140 – "Thy word is very pure: therefore thy servant loveth it."
- Psalm 119:142-143 – "Thy righteousness is an everlasting righteousness, and thy law is the truth. Trouble and anguish have taken hold on me: yet thy commandments are my delights."
- Psalm 119:165 – "Great peace have they which love thy law: and nothing shall offend them."

As Long As I Walk With God, I Will Always Have Hope

- Psalm 31:24 – "Be of good courage, and he shall strengthen your heart, all ye that hope in the Lord."
- Psalm 38:15 – "For in thee, O Lord, do I hope: thou wilt hear, O Lord my God."
- Psalm 42:5 – "Why art thou cast down, O my soul? and why art thou disquieted in me? hope thou in God: for I shall yet praise him for the help of his countenance."

- Psalm 42:11 – "Why art thou cast down, O my soul? and why art thou disquieted within me? hope thou in God: for I shall yet praise him, who is the health of my countenance, and my God."
- Psalm 43:5 – "Why art thou cast down, O my soul? and why art thou disquieted within me? hope in God: for I shall yet praise him, who is the health of my countenance, and my God."
- Psalm 70:14 – "But I will hope continually, and will yet praise thee more and more."

My Life Would Be Empty Without God

- Psalm 39:4-5 – "Lord, make me to know mine end, and the measure of my days, what it is; that I may know how frail I am. Behold, thou hast made my days as an handbreadth; and mine age is as nothing before thee: verily every man at his best state is altogether vanity. Selah."

I Can Develop Patience Through My Troubles

- Psalm 27:14 – "Wait on the Lord: be of good courage, and he shall strengthen thine heart: wait, I say on the Lord."
- Psalm 37:7-9 – "Rest in the Lord, and wait patiently for him: fret not thyself because of him who prospereth in his way, because of the man who bringeth wicked devices to pass. Cease from anger, and forsake wrath: fret not thyself in any wise to do evil. For evildoers shall be cut off: but those that wait upon the Lord, they shall inherit the earth."
- Psalm 45:10 – "Be still, and know that I am God: I will be exalted among the heathen, I will be exalted in the earth."
- Psalm 62:5 – "My soul, wait thou only upon God; for my expectation is from him."

My Mind Can Be at Ease

- Psalm 94:19 – "In the multitude of my thoughts within me thy comforts delight my soul."

In God I Have Found a Friend I Can Trust

- Psalm 56:3-4 – "What time I am afraid, I will trust in thee. In God will I praise his word, in God I have put my trust; I will not fear what flesh can do unto me."

- Psalm 56:11 – "In God have I put my trust: I will not be afraid what man can do unto me."
- Psalm 57:1 – "Be merciful unto me, O God, be merciful unto me: for my soul trusteth in thee: yea, in the shadow of thy wings will I make my refuge, until these calamities be overpast."
- Psalm 62:8 – "Trust in him at all times; ye people, pour out your heart before him: God is a refuge for us. Selah."
- Psalm 71:5 – "For thou art my hope, O Lord God: thou art my trust from my youth."

I Can Be Victorious Over All of Life's Troubles

- Psalm 41:11 – "By this I know that thou favourest me, because mine enemy doth not triumph over me."
- Psalm 64:10 – "The righteous shall be glad in the Lord, and shall trust in him; and all the upright in heart shall glory."
- Psalm 92:12-15 – "The righteous shall flourish like the palm tree: he shall grow like a cedar in Lebanon. Those that be planted in the house of the Lord shall flourish in the courts of our God. They shall still bring forth fruit in old age; they shall be fat and flourishing; to shew that the Lord is upright: he is my rock, and there is no unrighteousness in him."
- Psalm 116:15 – "Precious in the sight of the Lord is the death of his saints."
- Psalm 138:7 – "Though I walk I the midst of trouble, thou wilt revive me: thou shalt stretch forth thine hand against the wrath of mine enemies, and thy right hand shall save me."

The Lord is My Shepherd

- Psalm 23:1-6 – "The Lord is my shepherd; I shall not want. He maketh me to lie down in green pastures: he leadeth me beside the still waters. He restoreth my soul: he leadeth me in the paths of righteousness for his name's sake. Yea, though I walk through the valley of the shadow of death, I will fear no evil: for thou art with me; thy rod and thy staff they comfort me. Thou preparest a table before me in the presence of mine enemies: thou anointest my head with oil; my cup runneth over. Surely goodness and mercy shall follow me all the days of my life: and I will dwell in the house of the Lord for ever."

- Psalm 79:13 – "So we thy people and sheep of thy pasture will give thee thanks for ever: we will shew forth thy praise to all generations."
- Psalm 100:3 – "Know ye that the Lord he is God: it is he that hath made us, and not we ourselves; we are his people, and the sheep of his pasture."

Part Three

Personally Sitting in the Lap of God

Note: The following pages contain excerpts from a blog that Shannon and I maintained in the closing weeks of her life. She added her comments as she was able, sometimes dictating them to me. Several thousand people visited the blog during this time, some on numerous occasions. It was a great way for us to keep friends and family apprised of Shannon's condition. It was also a great outlet for dealing with the challenges we were facing. The blog is online in its entirety at www.acoupleconquerscancer.com. No money is made from the site. All are welcome to share it with those who might benefit from it. – mg

A Couple ~~Copes With~~ Conquers Cancer

Thursday, February 25, 2010
Conquering, Not Just Coping

As you can see from the graphic in the header, the idea for this site started with a focus on how we as a married couple have been coping with cancer. When I looked up the word, "coping" and found that it means, "to struggle or deal, esp. on fairly even terms or with some degree of success," I felt that the word was so bland. To me, the idea of coping with something means you're putting up with it. Well, I don't want to put up with cancer. I want to beat it into submission. I want to control it, not allow it to control me. In short, I want to conquer it.

The Key to Success (from Shannon)

The key to managing a challenge such as this is to stick together. There is no way I could possibly face the many doctor visits, pokes, prods, hospital stays, chemotherapy, and other trappings of cancer without a strong support system. That support begins with my husband of 30 years, who has never wavered in his love and strength. I draw from that strength to help me through each day.

Friday, February 26, 2010
"We"?

A lot of times I'll talk about how "we" are going through this. That may sound kind of strange. After all, Shannon is the one with the disease. I can't feel the pain she's experiencing, but I do feel pain. It just hurts in a different way. The emotional strain is the most challenging and from time to time that spills over into some physical pain. It's not really "sympathy pains" like a husband gets during his wife's labor. It's real pain. Casting this stress on God in prayer as He invites us to in I Peter 5:7 is my outlet for relief. When one is caring for a spouse with an illness, he or she needs to acknowledge the strain and take the necessary actions to deal with it so that they can have the physical strength to be there when their spouse needs them.

Saturday, February 27, 2010
Day One

Time now to fill in some blanks. May 27, 2009 was the day we first heard the word "cancer" and Shannon's name used in the same sentence. The two of us were alone in the car when she told me. I took the news calmly. My immediate reaction was to try to reassure her that everything would be okay. I believed that and, in fact, I still do.

Half an hour later I was breaking the news to our children. What caused that word to stick in my throat and be held back by tears at that point I'm not sure I'll ever know. Maybe it was a rush of memories of all of the years Shannon and I had had together with our children; maybe it was the mistaken notion that a diagnosis of cancer was an immediate death sentence; maybe it was looking into the eyes of my children and feeling the pain that I knew they would feel in just a few moments when the word finally came out of my mouth; maybe it was just having to say the word, "cancer." Whatever the cause, the word did not come easily.

Tears and hugs and reassurances came next, followed by frank talk of a practical plan for dealing with our new challenge. Our routine would be interrupted. There would be hospital stays forthcoming, treatments to take, medical equipment to which we would need to get accustomed. In effect, multiple changes were coming and could not be stopped.

When cancer comes, it doesn't sneak in gradually. It rushes in like a flood, bringing with it previously untouched emotions, untold challenges and an uncertain outcome.

Sunday, February 28, 2010
The Story Continues

In July 2009 we spent a few days (or years, depending on your perspective) at a hospital about an hour away. The surgery was successful but we were still facing cancer. By this time we were both thinking, "When is this nightmare going to be over?" Other than having four babies, Shannon had never had a hospital stay and I've never been an overnight patient in a hospital at any time in my life.

One thing you'd better learn in a hospital is patience, and you'd better learn it in a hurry. It's not anything like being at home. You can't run down to the refrigerator and grab a snack. Privacy is unheard of (and, by the way, 70% of the people who pass by an open hospital room door look in; 100% of those who look in think it's strange when an occupant in that room waves at them). Obviously the sleeping arrangements are different as are the smells, the sounds and even the television. It's a different world and BOTH the patient and spouse have to adapt.

Routines (from Shannon)

The day your diagnosis is listed as "cancer" is a day that is not easily forgotten. It seems as if your life is separated by a gulf; those days that happened before cancer, and then the days after. The challenge of fighting this disease permeates every pore, invades every thought.

It is easy to become overwhelmed by the everyday changes. New medications must be taken, many times to a confusing level of intricacy. Equipment might be needed, such as oxygen machinery or special monitoring devices. There are feelings of isolation, frustration, and exhaustion.

Eventually, one becomes familiar with what was once totally alien. The sound of the oxygen machine, while still loud, is now a familiar sound. The wires and tubes are organized, and the routine is set. The internet and the telephone help ward away the isolation, and big windows bring in lots of sunshine or snow or rain to bring variety to the day.

And then you can fight....and fight...and fight. Our motto has become, "Fight every day; enjoy every moment!"

Monday, March 1, 2010
The Next Chapter

The phrase, "the dog days of summer" took on a new meaning for us in August 2009. On Saturday, August 8 Shannon was at home and having difficulty breathing. I was going to drive her to the emergency room but when she could barely walk as far as the living room we decided to call the ambulance. Later we would discover that the cancer had spread to her lungs and had caused a hole in one of them that had it working at only 10% of its capacity. While in surgery a cancer-induced hole developed in the other lung. Thus began a string of 25 days in the hospital, interrupted by only a few days off back at home.

It was during this time that I experienced what was without a doubt the lowest point of my life. One day, struggling for a breath, Shannon said to me, "Take care of the kids." I knew her medications might be affecting her mood, but still, it felt like she was giving up. All I remember saying is, "I refuse to believe you're going to die from this. We will not lose." She had demonstrated such a strong will to that point; now she needed to borrow some of my determination. It was only fair that I lend it. After all, she had already given me so much of hers.

Wednesday, March 3, 2010
Finishing Up 2009

After our August/mid-September hospital ordeal, we fell into sort of a routine back at home. Granted, it was a routine different than we had ever experienced in our lives but it was a routine nonetheless. There were still rough days but the news that the chemotherapy was making a difference helped us deal with those. As the holidays approached we looked forward to the family being together. Even when December brought the news that this treatment had stopped working and that we would have to move on to another after the first of the year, we were still excited about the holidays. They gave us something to look forward to. We have found that to be important. Whether these things are large (the family coming together, going on a short trip) or small (bringing home a movie to watch together, cooking a favorite meal), the anticipation of positive events has helped us deal with the down times.

Saturday, March 6, 2010
Off Schedule

I'll admit to being "schedule happy." I like everything to be organized, in its proper place and just so. But cancer has its own schedule. For instance, while I had planned for the last few days to update the history of our encounter with this illness, one of the offshoots of the cancer decided to attack Shannon again and has brought her back to the hospital. Ideally, we were going to post here daily, each one of us playing off the other in our writing. She just hasn't had the strength and is barely able to talk, much less write.

Dealing with cancer requires flexibility. You go where you need to go and change what you need to change in order to accommodate the unexpected. Basically the whole experience is filled with unexpected twists and turns. While learning from those who have gone through this is helpful, no two experiences are exactly alike. Glean what you can from what others have to say, but don't be frustrated if things don't happen on the same time table as it did for them.

Sunday, March 7, 2010
Up to Date

To finish the timeline of our experience, I don't recall ever looking forward to a new year more than I looked forward to 2010. 2009 had had some other challenges beside the cancer so the prospect of a fresh start was pleasant. It was another of those "things to look forward to" that we tried to keep in front of us to help us keep going.

For the first six weeks of 2010 we went through the weekly treatment regimen, only briefly interrupted by a visit to the emergency room, not really knowing if any progress was being made. A scan on February 22 told us that, in fact, no progress had been made and the cancer was worsening. In addition, the scan revealed the lungs were again collapsing. A few hours after the scan we were again in the hospital and stayed for five days, only to come back again four days later with recurring issues related to the lungs as well as pneumonia that had developed.

So here we are in our third floor condo and now you are up to date. Several words come to mind in summarizing the past nine and a half months, among which are: unique, challenging, frightening, faith-building. Through it all though I can say that I can't think of a time when we lost hope. We've never really faced any long-term challenges in our lives. This is a first. All those years of studying God's inspired Word (the Bible) and committing it to heart and mind have, I'm convinced, built a wall around us that is protecting us from despair and doubt.

Monday, March 8, 2010
Riding the Roller Coaster

Roller coasters have never been a favorite of mine. I prefer to keep my stomach in one location. Dealing with cancer is a roller coaster ride of epic proportions. One day you're riding high when things seem to be going well. On another day you've been hurtled down literally into "the valley of the shadow of death," wondering if this is the last time you'll get to hold your spouse and see her sweet face this side of eternity. On still another day everything seems normal, like it was in the pre-cancer days. For me, an important factor in dealing with this is to maintain an even keel. Don't panic in the valleys. Don't become unrealistic at the peaks. Stay steady and enjoy the time you have with your loved one, caressing every moment you have together as if it were the last. (Actually, why should we wait for a long-term illness to make us appreciate life's precious moments?)

The last two days have been good ones as we wait for the pneumonia to go away while anticipating surgical repair of Shannon's lungs. With the completion of these two steps, we can move on to the next treatment in hopes that this will be the one that sends the cancer into remission.

Wednesday, March 10, 2010
Peace That Passes All Understanding

So far, so good on today's surgery. The pneumonia skirmish and now the lung skirmish still occupy us and are keeping us from fighting the bigger battle of cancer. Thankfully we're beating back these enemies so it is with high hopes that we prepare to take on the major adversary within the next week to ten days.

With each challenge we've faced we have seen Bible verses come to life. Verses such as Philippians 4:6-7 (I'm going to make you get your Bible and look those up) have always been meaningful and powerful because the Bible is God's living Word (Hebrews 4:12), but here, in a surgery pre-op room, I actually see the peace that passes all understanding in Shannon's eyes. This is not a tumultuous time for either of us. Instead, it's an opportunity for us to enjoy God's blessings.

Saturday, March 13, 2010
A Little Courtesy

Even though we're in that "hurry up and wait" mode, the last couple of days have been peaceful. Shannon is eating well, breathing well and, aside from the napping that comes along with the pain medication, is in many ways back to herself. I knew things were bad a week or so ago when she said she didn't want any chocolate. Thankfully, she's eaten everything chocolate I've brought to her lately.

From our youth we've known the value of courtesy. Having spent little time in the hospital, I'm nonetheless aware of the challenges and pressures faced by the staff. Some time ago I remember reading something that suggested the hospital staff appreciates "please" and "thank you." It may not be much but we've tried to use those words as often as possible during our stays. The doctors, nurses and the rest of the crew put in a lot of work. We've struck up conversations with just about all of them. It seems that just a little common courtesy from a patient might make their jobs more enjoyable.

Tuesday, March 16, 2010
Up For a Bit of Air (from Shannon)

The past week has been a blur of procedures and fevers and medications. I'm feeling better today, and am happy to be enjoying this lovely day.

I am so blessed, with family and friends, who encourage me to keep fighting. I will!

Monday, March 22, 2010
Home Again

Last Wednesday, all things were go for leaving the hospital. I had gone to pick up a prescription, our boys were waiting in the hallway outside of Shannon's room and she was inside preparing to dress, sign discharge papers and leave. Suddenly she lost a significant amount of blood and passed out. The nurses revived her but by the next morning she was in surgery again, this time in an effort to stop the incessant bleeding she has been experiencing for so many months. A day or two prior to all of this we thought again that we might be going home but a very dangerous attack came then as well and, thankfully, soon went. When Friday came and they released us, we were watching every step to make sure this time our departure would come to pass. Her many continuous days in the bed weakened her leg muscles but her determination had her quickly adjusting and she is now getting around with the help of a walker. She is eating and resting well and we look forward to being able to once again attack the source of all of this, the cancer.

The Psalmist wrote, "I will praise thee; for I am fearfully and wonderfully made…" (Psalm 139:14). The complexity of the human body has never been so evident to me as it is now. Our bodies are so intricate that, while the vast majority of our muscles, cells, etc. are working properly, one tiny afflicted area can stop us in our tracks. That's not always bad. In this case, had we gotten home on Wednesday and had Shannon lost the blood and passed out at home instead of in the hospital, the results could have been much worse. At the time we were disappointed that we were not going home, but the cause of our disappointment actually turned out to be a blessing. I may sound like my needle is stuck in a groove (that's "record" talk for you younger folks) but you really don't want to get too bound up in a schedule when dealing with cancer. Circumstances can change in an instant.

Tuesday, March 23, 2010
Normal (from Shannon)

The definition of "normal" changes often during this type of challenge. Normal, a year ago, meant shopping trips, visits with friends, and lots of church activities. Normal, today, means taking meds, resting, visiting assorted doctors, and rebuilding strength.

It's important to me to have something that feels really "Normal". My online classes have been my "normal" thing to do. It takes me away from the IVs, the strong medicines, and the odd smells that come with this.

I must admit, I'm impatient. I want to be outside, smelling those hyacinths and feeling the fresh air. I want to visit with friends, and attend every church activity possible. These things will come; I must be patient. In the meantime, redefining normal is a daily process.

Thursday, March 25, 2010
Another Bend in the Road

It's been such a joy to be home. Tomorrow we make our way back to the hospital for another surgery. We're in that vicious cycle of trying to fight the cancer but being prohibited by other complications that are being caused by the cancer. The apostle Paul wrote, "We are troubled on every side, yet not distressed; we are perplexed, but not in despair." (II Corinthians 4:8). The battle is getting tougher. How anyone can face death without the faith that comes from God's written Word is hard to imagine. The Bible gives us plenty of examples of men and women of faith. It's my privilege to be able to see a living example of faith in Shannon every day.

Saturday, March 27, 2010
A Time For Appreciation

Today we were told that the surgery we were expecting to have is not necessary at this time. On Tuesday we expect to have the other chest tube removed. We're thankful for every positive step. We're trying to make sure that we don't spend so much time asking that we forget to give thanks.

Wednesday, March 31, 2010
I Don't Know What to Say

Yesterday Shannon had a radiation treatment, its purpose being to lessen and hopefully eliminate her blood loss. Today brings with it the typical side effects but her temperature has been normal for two days so that good news offsets the harshness of the radiation. She says she's not in pain, just weak. She always has enough strength for a sweet smile when I need one though. I've burned that look into my mind for the past 31 plus years that we've known each other and carry it with me.

Many times people don't know what to say to folks in a situation like ours. A feeling of inadequacy gnaws at them as they avoid saying anything for fear of saying the wrong thing. That lack of communication then turns to guilt for not talking at all to the sufferers. It's a vicious cycle. If you've ever had this happen to you, allow me to help you out. Say, "I'm sorry," "I'm thinking of you and praying for you," "I love you," "I want you to know how much you mean to me." These are simple, few word statements. After saying the one or ones of your choosing, sit back and listen. Don't probe. Just listen. Let that person lead the conversation. Whether you're talking by phone or in person, you don't have to keep the conversation going for a long time. Just knowing that they are in someone's heart is sufficient for most people dealing with a critical illness.

Friday, April 2, 2010
Two Steps Ahead, A Brief Step Back

For the first time since last August, Shannon is breathing without the aid of an oxygen machine or tank. The work that was done in repairing her lungs was apparently successful. The cancer had traveled there through lymph nodes and caused damage. The tumors continue to grow in the lungs but we're hoping to get to another chemotherapy treatment to see if it can help.

We're still in the hospital due to Shannon's persistent fever. It's just a couple or a few degrees over normal, but when we're talking about body temperature that small range can be a huge factor in one's health. Sometimes it's the seemingly tiniest things that can slow you down. More positives than negatives today though.

Saturday, April 3, 2010
Making the Hard Choices

Throughout our battle with this illness, we've found ourselves faced with challenging choices. None was more challenging than today. When we learned earlier in the week that our daughter, Whitney and grandson, Daniel would be coming today for a week's visit, we set our hearts on getting home so that we could spend time with them. Based on the fever that just doesn't want to go away, the doctors informed us that they had different plans if we still wanted to try to get a chemotherapy treatment and take advantage of the 20-30% chance they say we have of this treatment working. They felt that the best way to be prepared for the treatment would be for Shannon to be under constant care in the hospital. Home health care would be available if we went home, but of course it would not be available 24/7 like it is in the hospital.

So here we were, on one hand wanting to spend quality time with our family members who had flown half way across the country, and on the other hand wanting to at least get a shot at the treatment that we have not been able to take due to one reason or another for so many months. If the treatment has such a small chance of being effective, would it be best to just go on home and enjoy the family in a more familiar environment? If the treatment has any chance at all of being effective, no matter how slim that chance may be, would it be best to stay in the hospital, sacrificing that week of family time for the hope of having many more weeks of family time in the future?

We opted for the prolonged stay in the hospital. Since the element of risk is evident on all sides, we decided to go the route of doing whatever we can to get to the treatment and hope and pray that the 20-30% chance is enough. Talking things out with one another and with the doctors seems to be key to making the hard choices.

Sunday, April 4, 2010
Sometimes the Choices Are Made For You

Yesterday's difficult decision turned into a non-decision today as the doctors informed us that the cancer is now untreatable. While a chemotherapy treatment could still be an option, the scans show that the tumors are growing so rapidly that a treatment would virtually be of no effect and would in fact make Shannon feel worse.

So now we go home to familiar surroundings, hoping to make her comfortable. She's not in pain, just getting weaker. She's also not afraid. This is "the valley of the shadow of death" of which the Psalmist wrote in Psalm 23:4. We both know the Shepherd of this Psalm and right now we are walking beside Him, hand in hand. Soon I'll need to let go but Shannon will continue her walk through the valley, not alone, but in the presence of the one who can safely lead her home.

Monday, April 5, 2010
From Shannon

Despite the disappointment of knowing that medical treatment is no longer effective, I am thankful. I am thankful for the many friends who have expressed their love and concern for me, for my family who has been so supportive through this ordeal and particularly, I am thankful for my husband who has been my strength.

God is good. I know He will take care of me and I know He will take care of those I leave behind.

Tuesday, April 6, 2010
Just Another Ordinary, Everyday Love Story - Part 1

For over 30 years I have been married to my best friend. Occasionally someone will comment on the longevity of our relationship and wonder how we've done it. If you'll indulge me a little meandering down memory lane, I'd like to share how Shannon and I got to this point in our lives where, as a single-minded force, we have been able to stare down cancer and conquer it. (Yes, conquer it. Even though it will eventually claim Shannon's life, cancer has not defeated us. If its intention was to discourage us and cause us to grow apart due to the stress and strain it causes, it has failed miserably. We have only become stronger and closer as a result of this.)

When we first met at fine arts camp in Henderson, TN in 1978, we didn't like each other very much. I was the new kid in town and she thought I was a dumb athlete (she always has been good at judging character). She was very sure of herself, had been a part of that group for a couple of years and held some leadership positions. I thought she was snooty. A week or so later, in my first semester at Freed-Hardeman University, I had pretty much forgotten about her, choosing instead to focus on getting acquainted with other people at the school as well as my new surroundings.

Sometime into the semester the drama department was holding auditions for "The Music Man." I tried out and won a small role. You can probably imagine who the student director was - Shannon. At that point our opinions of each other had not changed, but as days of rehearsals passed, I began to notice something about her. I again saw that self-assurance, but this time in a different light. I saw it even in the face of a bunch of male teenage cast members who sometimes weren't very respectful of their young, female leader. I also saw an interest in and concern for other people. There was something there that I had never really seen before in a young lady and suddenly I wanted to get to know her better.

I asked her out and, thankfully, she agreed to go with me to dinner at The Old Country Store in Jackson, TN and then to Bible class afterwards. It was a memorable evening for me. Does that mean I remember all the details? Well, I recall where we sat but if you ask me what I ate and what she ate, forget about it. Regarding the meal itself, suffice it to say that we ate food, got full, I paid the check and we left. But this person for whom I previously had little regard had now captured my thoughts, and, as I would soon find out, my heart.

More to come...

Wednesday, April 7, 2010
Shannon's Turn

Coming home has been bittersweet. While I am thrilled to be back in familiar surroundings and away from the sterile atmosphere of the hospital, I know that this will be the last place on earth I will live. However, doesn't it seem more appropriate to go from the home that has given me joy and pleasure for so many years directly into the home for which I've waited all my life?

I will be leaving one set of loving hands to go to another. I am not afraid, I'm in no pain and I'm thankful to still have a clear enough brain to be able to enjoy my family. I love you all.

Just Another Ordinary, Everyday Love Story - Part 2

I am the world's fastest shopper. When I see what I like, I get it. I've always been that way. So maybe it shouldn't come as a surprise that after our first date and six more days of seeing and getting to know Shannon, I asked her to marry me. That's right, it took me a whole week to muster the courage to ask her to be my wife. When people say that you'll "just know" when you find the right one, they are right, at least in my case. A little more than a year later we were married. Shannon was dressed in a beautiful white gown that she had made on the sewing machine I had bought her for her birthday. Not being a person who readily shows his emotions, I nonetheless cried throughout the ceremony, not so much out of nervousness as out of gratitude for and amazement at the gift God had given me.

When I say that ours is just another ordinary, everyday love story, I mean just that. Our life together has had very little drama. We have never been on the brink of marital collapse. We have both been faithful to each other and to the vows we made in the sight of God. Our children have been outstanding and continue to faithfully serve God as Christians. Basically, if I were to write our story in a book I probably couldn't pay people to take the copies. Our life is just not "Hollywood" enough.

In spite of how mundane our life might appear to some, it has been filled with constant open communication, mutual respect and love for one another and for God. Just as a person is not fully grown on the day of his birth, a marriage is not fully grown right after the "I Do's" are said. To use another metaphor, marriage is a house constantly under construction, never completed until one of the spouses leaves this life.

Now we come to this, the final chapter of our story. Each challenge we've faced, each prayer we've prayed, each Bible verse we've read, each midnight heart-to-heart, each tear and each success we've experienced over 30+ years have made this past year and its many challenges seem, as the apostle Paul said, like a "light affliction." (II Corinthians 4:17). To get to this point we really haven't done anything that any other married couple can't themselves do. Devotion to God and commitment to one another as husband and wife are attainable by all.

Friday, April 9, 2010
When Love Takes Over

When we learned that Shannon's cancer was untreatable we had yet another decision to make. Should we stay in the hospital with 24/7 care or go home with the assistance of hospice? Frankly, to me it was not ever in question that we would go home. Who doesn't want to be home? However, Shannon was concerned that she would be a burden. I imagine that this is not uncommon among those in her situation and that it can become a nagging feeling, despite constant reassurances to the contrary.

Since being home I've learned some valuable new skills as a caregiver. I've also developed a heightened appreciation for all those men and women who tended to Shannon in the hospital. Whether they were administering medicine, changing sheets or whatever, those who give their lives to serving in medical care are wonderful people. No job that they do is unimportant.

The role that I have now assumed has allowed me to plumb the depths of my love for Shannon and, as I have done so I find that it is as deep as I always felt it was. None of the tasks I now do for her is burdensome in the least. I'm sure the most difficult task will be that of finally letting her go, although I'll never let her out of my heart.

Saturday, April 10, 2010
Planning Ahead

Among the difficult tasks I've encountered in the past week is that of preparing for my life without Shannon. Like a lot of people, we've planned for our deaths with wills, insurance, etc., but in the planning stages, death seems so far away. There's a considerable difference between the preparation for and the practical application of the deeds and events surrounding the death of one's spouse. The former is "way off in the distance" (or so we think), while the latter is staring you right in the face.

For over 30 years I've relied on Shannon to help me organize the many facets of our life together. Ironically, I am now relying on her to help me organize my life without her. Whether I'm asking her where something is or how to do something that she had typically done, I'm thankful for her patient answers. I'm also thankful to know that, even though there will be a major void in my life after she's gone, the example she set in life will continue to influence me as I'm sure it will those whose lives she has touched.

Sunday, April 11, 2010
Enjoying the Moments

Over the 31+ years that we have known each other, Shannon and I have written memories that would fill a library full of books. We've never been ones to sit around and dwell in the past though. Sure, we've taken the pictures and filmed the significant events, but we rarely sit down and relive those memories. I guess it's because we're too busy in the present making more memories.

Interestingly enough, even now we're continuing this pattern. While we've been admiring old family photos and home movies from time to time since coming home, we still spend her waking minutes talking about our family as they are now, our friends, current events and God's faithfulness to us during this time. In short, we seem to be enjoying the moments we have together just as we always have without an overemphasis on the past or the future. Sometimes it's difficult to look into her eyes and not project myself into my future without her, but the effort to save that for my "private time" is well worth it and allows me to get the most out of this time that we have together.

Monday, April 12, 2010
Appropriate Scriptures

Shannon continues to battle bravely each day but she is getting weaker as the doctors said she would. She has minimal pain but other than the occasional Tylenol to ease her fevers, she takes no pain medication. She speaks openly to me of what is going on inside her and though it's difficult to hear, I know I need to be aware of it so that I can be the most help to her.

Several people who have contacted us have cited the qualities of the virtuous woman of Proverbs 31 as an appropriate description of Shannon's life. I feel the same way, considering verse 30 to be especially accurate. "Favour is deceitful, and beauty is vain: but a woman that feareth the Lord, she shall be praised." In this case I have been triply blessed in that while I found a lady who fears the Lord, I also know her to be charming and beautiful.

Another section of God's Word that comes to mind when I think of Shannon is Acts 9:36-41 where we read of Tabitha, also called Dorcas. Read those verses for yourself, especially verse 39, and see if you don't picture in your mind's eye the countless number of women who could stand around Shannon, holding out garments that she made or that she helped others make.

The Divinely inspired verse that really stands out to me though is the one that I know will apply to her for years after her passing. The apostle Paul wrote of Abel's righteousness, saying, "by it he being dead yet speaketh." (Hebrews 11:4). I am confident that Shannon will live on in the hearts of those she touched through sewing, through her Bible class teaching, through her loyal friendship and through her Christ-like example. Even now she shares smiles with those who see her and talk to her. I believe all who know her will carry a piece of her in their hearts and will benefit greatly as a result.

Tuesday, April 13, 2010
My Energizer Bunny

Here's your word for the day: Indomitable. Look it up, and if you don't see a picture of Shannon next to the definition then you have a faulty dictionary.

As visitors have come by in the last week, some have talked about items that they are sewing or quilting. As you might have guessed, somewhere in those conversations Shannon has been sharing tips to help those folks complete their projects. The apostle Paul quoted Jesus as saying, "It is more blessed to give than to receive." (Acts 20:35). I have to smile as I watch Shannon continuing to give of herself even in her weakened condition.

She's having a good day and has eaten more today than she has in several days. As always, we enjoy these days and are thankful for them.

Thursday, April 15, 2010
Going Against the Grain

As expected, Shannon is sleeping more. We seem to have the right mix of medications going so when she's awake she is alert. She's having some pain but we're able to lessen it before it gets too severe.

I'll have to admit that I'm blazing some new trails for myself here. In the past, whenever Shannon got sick I knew my job was to make sure she got what she needed so that she would get back to full health. Now, because she is not expected to recover, I can't do anything to help her get better. I can only make her comfortable and try to ease her pain. Initially it was difficult to accept this because one's basic nature is to help an ill loved one recover. Now that I have a better understanding of my role, I realize that by seeing to her comfort, I am helping her as much as I ever have.

Friday, April 16, 2010
Talk About Priceless

Remember the "priceless" credit card commercials? Glancing over at Shannon to discover that she has been gazing at me and smiling; catching that gleam in her eye that makes my heart melt; sharing a look that only those who have ever truly been in love can understand - now that's priceless.

She's had another good day today, eating well, resting well and enjoying occasional, brief visits. I'm glad we decided to come home and I'm thankful for our friends and family who have helped make this time so pleasurable. They're the best.

Saturday, April 17, 2010
Celebrate the Simple Pleasures

By her actions, Shannon is reminding me on a daily basis of the importance of the little things in life. She was so excited the other day because the swelling in her feet had gone down and she could move her toes. Today it was biscuits, gravy and sausage from Ross' Diner that brightened her morning. You ought to see her light up when she gets a piece of fresh fruit. For so many months during the chemotherapy she wasn't allowed to have it and now with every bite it seems as though she's tasting it for the first time.

In the Sermon on the Mount, Jesus told His audience to "behold the fowls of the air" and "consider the lilies of the field" to learn a lesson about God's care for His people (Matthew 6:26,28). These are just simple, every day things, but like so many other facets of God's creation, they can elicit joy and appreciation in the hearts of those who are willing to slow down for a moment or two and take a look at them.

Shannon has had another good day today and continues to share her smiles.

Sunday, April 18, 2010
Homecoming

This evening at 8:59 p.m. Eastern time, Shannon went home to be with the Lord. She was not in any pain and was surrounded by loved ones. As you would expect of her if you knew her, her final words were those of encouragement, telling us how much she loved us and how happy her life had been.

Shannon's life was one well-lived. With faith in God and love for others, she touched so many people across the globe. It was my blessed privilege to be her husband since December 30, 1979. I can't begin to imagine what my life would have been without her. She made my time here so joyful. There wasn't any challenge that we weren't able to overcome together, including this one.

The title of this site is "A Couple Conquers Cancer." As a faithful Christian, Shannon conquered it. It robbed her of her physical strength, but never of her determination. It stole her mobility, but not her heart. It even deprived her of her beautiful hair, but it did not touch her dignity. The Bible says in I Corinthians 15:57, "But thanks be to God, which giveth us the victory through our Lord Jesus Christ." This evening, Shannon became the victor and nothing harmful will ever bother her again (Revelation 21:4).

Where Was God?

(Note: I wrote the following soon after Shannon's passing. It was printed in the program that was handed out at her memorial service. - mg)

When facing life's trials, some begin to wonder if God is really there or, if He is, if He really cares about our suffering. Considering our frailty, such questioning is reasonable, so long as one searches for the answer and doesn't just throw his hands up in disgust and conclude that God does not exist. Job, Habakkuk, Asaph (Psalm 73) and others engaged in this type of thinking when they were facing difficulties. As we consider the question in this article's title, I hope that you will indulge me in my personal references. Their usage is the best way I know of providing an answer.

Where was God…

- …when we learned that my wife, Shannon had an aggressive cancer that had arisen suddenly and without warning?
- … when she nearly died of collapsed lungs caused by the cancer?
- … when our family was thrown into turmoil with emergency room visits followed by days and then weeks of hospital stays?
- … when we were told that the cancer was incurable and that the best we could aim for was to make her comfortable in her declining days?
- … when she lost her battle for life?
- … when she departed this world?

Now let me tell you where He was…

- …when we were told of her disease. He was in the same place as He had been the dozens of times in years past that she had previously gone to doctors for checkups and was pronounced healthy.
- …when she nearly died. He was in the same place as the day the world was blessed with her birth.

- …when we were experiencing the long days and nights of hospital stays. He was in the same place that He had been on the thousands of days in which we walked freely and in good health.
- … when we were told that the end for her was near. He was in the same place as He was the day that we fell in love and our world began.
- … when she lost her battle for life. He was in the same place that He was on the day that He gave His only begotten Son on the cross so that death would not have the victory over His faithful ones (I Corinthians 15:55-58)
- … when she departed this world. He was in the same place that He was when He welcomed her into His family by virtue of her new birth in immersion in water for the forgiveness of sins (Ephesians 3:15; John 3:3,5).

In essence, the God whom some blame for their woes when they're in the throes of life's challenges is the same God who is often forgotten when things are going well. He has not moved. The apostle Paul said that He is not far from every one of us, adding, "For in him we live, and move, and have our being (Acts 17:27-28). Through that same apostle God said, "I will never leave thee, nor forsake thee." (Hebrews 13:5). If in our trials we feel that God is not there it would be wise for us to consider the fact that it is we who have moved, not God. In life's darkness, thinking that God has forgotten us, we might find ourselves asking, "God, where are you?" but in life's good days, when we tend to forget God, perhaps He asks, "My child, where are you?"

Appendix
God's Plan of Salvation

.

God's Plan of Salvation

The Bible teaches that you and I are sinners (Romans 3:10,23). As such, we are displeasing to God (Psalm 5:5). Our sins, like a brick wall, separate us from Jehovah (Isaiah 59:1,2). They separate us from the one who is going to judge this world, the one who has the power to cast us into eternal hell or take us into eternal glory in heaven at Judgment (Matthew 7:21-23; 25:31-46).

Certainly all of us desire to avoid the punishment of hell and to go to heaven, but how can we accomplish this desire if we are sinners who stand separated from God? Were it not for the grace of God, we could not accomplish it at all (Matthew 19:25,26; Titus 2:11).

Ephesians 2:8 states, *"For by grace are ye saved through faith; and that not of yourselves: it is the gift of God."* That *"gift of God"* is *"eternal life through Jesus Christ our Lord."* (Romans 6:23). Prompted by His perfect love, God gave His only begotten Son, Jesus the Christ, as a sacrifice for our sins (John 3:16). The penalty for sin has to be paid. Because of God's grace and love, He does not want us to have to pay that penalty (though we hasten to mention that God's perfect justice demands that those who do not obey the Lord be punished – Deuteronomy 32:4; II Thessalonians 1:7-9). The blood of His Son that was shed on a cross on the hill of Calvary nearly 2000 years ago paid the price for sin.

Our sins CAN be forgiven. We CAN be pure in the sight of God IF we will be washed in the soul-saving blood of Christ that is made available to every sinner. But how are we washed in this blood? God's grace saves us, but His grace alone does not save. It is by His grace that everyone has the opportunity to be saved and it is by His grace that some will be saved, but not everyone will be saved in eternity (Matthew 7:13,14). Only those who obey the Lord's Gospel and thus are washed in the blood of Christ have the hope of eternal life (Revelation 1:5).

Again referring to Ephesians 2:8, we learn that faith plays a part in our salvation. By His grace, God provides salvation but WE must do something to receive it. We must believe (have faith) not only in Him (Hebrews 11:6), but also in Jesus as the Christ, the Son of God (John 8:24). BUT, faith alone is not sufficient to save us from our sins (James 2:24). James 2:19 says that the devils believe, but they are not saved. Faith that is not put into action is a dead faith that is useless (James 2:20).

The New Testament very clearly tells us how to act on our faith so as to secure the blessing of forgiveness of sins. With the faith that we gained from God's Word, the Bible, firmly planted in our hearts and minds (Romans 10:17), we learn from the Bible of our sinful state. Knowing that we don't want to continue our lives as lost sinners, the next logical step for us to take is repentance. To repent means to change one's direction, to turn from one's devotion to Satan and turn to a devotion to God. Jesus stated that we all MUST repent (Luke 13:3). Peter indicated the same in Acts 2:38 and 3:19.

Faith and repentance are still not enough to secure Divine forgiveness. In the New Testament book of Acts, sometimes called the book of conversions, we have an example of a believing, penitent sinner making a public confession of Christ. "*I believe that Jesus Christ is the Son of God,*" he declared. (Acts 8:37). Jesus had earlier stated that confession of belief in Him was necessary (Matthew 10:32,33). The apostle Paul later wrote that confession is made unto (in order to receive) salvation, "*for the scripture saith, Whosoever believeth on him shall not be ashamed.*" (Romans 10:10,11).

Faith, repentance and confession still fall short of the blood of Christ. II Timothy 2:10 says that salvation is IN Christ Jesus. The alien sinner has to get INTO Christ somehow, but nowhere does the Bible say that we can believe into Christ. Nowhere does Sacred Scripture tell us that we can repent into Christ. The Divine record contains not one statement that says we can confess into Christ. How then can we get into Christ and be washed in the soul-cleansing blood of the Lamb of God (Hebrews 9:13,14)?

One passage of the Bible answers this question for us. Galatians 3:27 speaks of people who had been baptized (immersed) INTO Christ. Verse 28 speaks of them being IN Christ Jesus. They got there by virtue of their immersion into Christ.

The absolute necessity of immersion to be saved is taught in several New Testament passages (Mark 16:16; Acts 2:38; Acts 22:16; Romans 6:3ff; I Peter 3:21). This immersion is to be the one authorized by the Father, the Son and the Holy Spirit in God's Word (Matthew 28:19). It is the one immersion mentioned in Ephesians 4:4-6, namely, immersion in water for the forgiveness of sins through the blood of Christ.

Faith, repentance, confession and immersion for the remission of sins form man's part of being saved. These are not man-made works, for no one shall be saved by works that man creates (Ephesians 2:9). These are acts of obedience that God has mandated in His Word, acts that we MUST do if we want to break down the wall of sin that stands between us and Him.

Following these steps of salvation and rising up from the waters of immersion, not only is one a new creature (II Corinthians 5:17), but he is then a member of the Lord's church, the one and ONLY one Jesus promised to build (Matthew 16:18). The Lord adds the saved to the church (Acts 2:47).

His church is not a denomination but is the one body into which all who want to be saved in eternity must come (Ephesians 1:22,23; 4:4-6; 5:23). Only those who have obeyed the Gospel and thus become members of the Lord's church can be called Christians (Acts 11:26).

Won't you, dear reader, look at the scriptures that have been cited, examine them carefully and let them sink deeply into your heart? Won't you then muster the courage to obey the Lord? Your sins will be washed away, you will become a servant of the Lord (Romans 6:17,18) and a part of His family (Ephesians 3:10-15) and you will have the hope of eternal life (Titus 1:1,2; I John 2:25), a hope that will become reality in Judgment if you will only continue to follow the Word of God exclusively all the days of your Christian life on earth (II Timothy 4:7,8; Hebrews 10:36). May God bless you as you do His will.

Other Titles From Hopkins Publishing

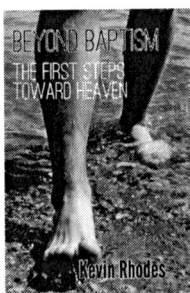

Beyond Baptism

Integrate new Christians into the congregation, strengthen their faith, and help them become active as Christians!

Building Blocks of Faith

This sequel to Beyond Baptism, which still stands on its own, walks through thirteen topics to ground Christians in the faith and correct common misunderstandings.

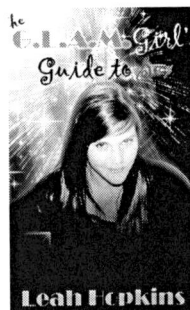

THE GLAM GIRL'S GUIDE TO SEX

This straight forward study breaks down what a girl is going through as she matures and offers biblical guidance as she contemplates decisions that affect her opinions, actions and most importantly the destination of her soul.

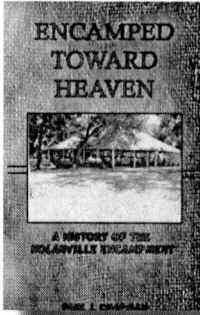

Encamped Toward Heaven

The Nolanville church of Christ Encampment was born during a time of spiritual revival in America, and eventually grew to be one of the most well-known and enduring annual camp meetings in Central Texas. Encamped Toward Heaven tells the story of the pioneer families who established the Lord's church on the banks of Nolan Creek.

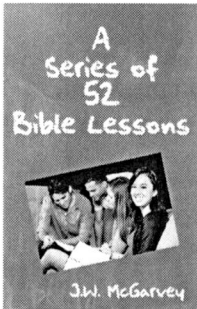

A SERIES OF 52 BIBLE LESSONS

J.W. McGarvey prvoides an excellent resource: one full year of curriculum for the Bible class program or home devotional studies for the serious Bible Student.

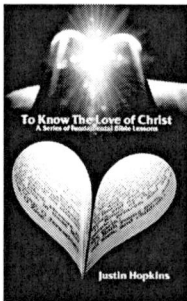

To Know The Love of Christ

A series of Bible studies which teach the fundamentals of New Testament Christianity They can be used as an evangelistic tool, or as a personal course of study.

Annual Southwest Bible Lectures

Each volume contains two quarters of material for Bible class curriculum, with concise lessons and thought provoking questions.
Books from previous years are also available!

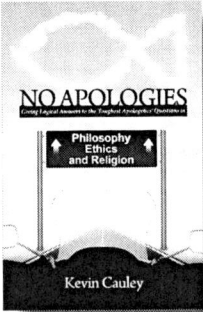

No Apologies

Kevin Cauley provides the Lord's church with a useful resource in the field of Christian Evidences by presenting the case for Christian faith in a manner that is both thorough and understandable.

Speaking From The Heart

This is a one year devotional guide, written by members of the Karns Church of Christ in Knoxville, TN. The articles are intended to uplift our spirits and challenge our attitudes and actions to be more closely conformed to the image of Jesus.

Singled Out

An enriching study for young women designed to help you find identity and contentment in your relationship with God whether or not you have found a spouse.

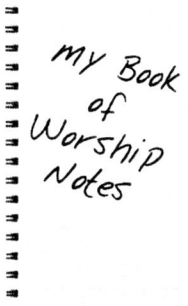

My Book of Worship Notes

This book of note pages provides space to take notes in worship for one solid year. Now your kids can listen to the sermon, take notes, write down scripture refrences, and draw a personal application of the lesson.

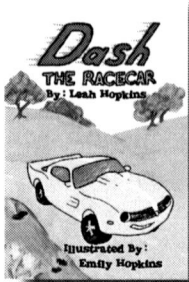

DASH THE RACECAR

Come join Dash as he commits to the race of a lifetime, and see how you can get the greatest prize of all... eternity with Jesus!!!

THE BEST PLACE TO LAY AN EGG

In a lively and whimsical way, Emily Hopkins takes you into the minds of a bunch of hens...

JOHNNY HAD A DOLLAR

Johnny has a dollar. Now the question is what to do with it? As this young boy considers all the many things he could do, he tries to decide what would be best.

Alphabear

From the author of Johnny Had A Dollar, comes a delightful way to teach young children how to alphabetize.

CPSIA information can be obtained at www.ICGtesting.com
Printed in the USA
LVOW10s0537050813

346254LV00007B/246/P

9 781620 809754